Style & Strategy

Answer Key

Michele Poff, PhD

© 2025 Michele Poff

All rights reserved.

No portion of this book may be reproduced in any form without written permission from the publisher or author, except as permitted by US copyright laws.

Accomplish Publishing

Ordering information: michele@accomplishcomm.com

Book cover by author

ISBN:

Answer Key paperback	978-1-941162-12-5
	978-1-941162-18-7

Related ISBNs

Style & Strategy ebook	978-1-941162-09-5
Style & Strategy Answer Key ebook	978-1-941162-10-1
Style & Strategy paperback	978-1-941162-11-8

Contents

1. Capitalization 1
2. Artefact Titles 1
3. Possessive Singular 1
4. Possessive Plural 2

Quiz 1 3

5. Commas and Semicolons in a List 4
6. Appositives 5
7. Its/it's; Whose/who's 6
8. Hyphenation & Modifier Construction 7

Quiz 2 8

9. Parallel Structure 9
10. Be Consistent 9
11. Sentence Grammar 10
12. Comma Before the Main Clause 11
13. Joining Clauses 12
14. Run-ons and Fragments 13
15. Keep Related Words Together 13
16. Don't Dangle the Modifier 14

Grammar Exam 14

17. *Be* Verbs 15
18. Avoid Negation 15
19. Delete Unnecessary Words 16

Quiz 3 16

20. Paragraph Cohesiveness 17
21. Paragraph Structure 17
22. Transitions 19

Quiz 4 19

23. First Words Matter 20
24. The End-Weight Principle 21

25.	Prepositional Phrases are Mobile Modifiers	21
26.	Vary Sentences	25
27.	Quantity as a Rhetorical Tool	25
28.	Strategic Word Choice	26

Quiz 5 26

Composition Quiz 27

Grammar and Composition Exam 28

Genres 29

    Academic Writing 30

    Analytical Writing 32

    Blog Paragraph 34

    Business Writing 36

    Copywriting 38

    Creative Writing 40

    Descriptive Writing 42

    Expository Writing 44

    Journalistic Writing 46

    Narrative Writing 48

    Oral Presentation Script 50

    Personal Writing 52

    Persuasive Writing 54

    Review Writing 56

    Script Writing 58

    Summary 60

    Technical Writing 62

    Travel Writing 64

29.		logos, ethos, and pathos	74
	A.	strong logos, weak ethos, weak pathos	74
	B.	weak logos, strong ethos, weak pathos	75

	C.	weak logos, weak ethos, strong pathos 75
	D.	strong logos, strong ethos, weak pathos 76
	E.	weak logos, strong ethos, strong pathos 77
	F.	strong logos, weak ethos, strong pathos 79
	G.	strong logos, strong ethos, strong pathos 80
	H.	weak logos, weak ethos, weak pathos 82
30.	Essential Argument Elements 84	
31.	Additional Argument Elements 85	
32.	Oral Presentation Structure 89	
35.	Relevant Visual on Each Slide 91	
36.	The 3-5 Rule 91	
37.	Aristotle's Trilogy 93	

1. Capitalization
    1. My ~~M~~mom helps me a lot.
    2. Justin is a manager at the ~~B~~bank on the corner.
    3. Frieda works at a small ~~C~~company called ~~t~~The ~~s~~Sandy ~~f~~Foot.
    4. Johann's ~~A~~aunt is a well-known ~~A~~artist.
    5. A grandfather clock takes up a lot of space but sounds so beautiful. (no change)
    6. Xiao drives an ~~E~~elite ~~M~~model ~~C~~car.
    7. The Valliens said their favorite part of their ~~a~~Africa tour was the ~~S~~safari.
    8. The boys love to visit the local ~~S~~skate ~~P~~park, called Skate Away Skate Park, after ~~S~~school.
    9. How wide do you think the Amazon ~~r~~River is?
    10. The kids attended Washington University, the ~~U~~university in town.

2. Artefact Titles
    1. Ironically, Charlotte's daughter's favorite book is *Charlotte's Web*.
    2. When they went into the city, they caught a production of *Hamilton*.
    3. Jeremy's favorite film of all time is *Gone with the Wind*.
    4. Have you read the article called "Let's Get Serious" in the *New Yorker*?
    5. When you want to buy something new, it's still a good idea to check with *Consumer Reports*.
    6. The Kelly blue book value on that vehicle is $4,800. (no change)
    7. Nicki has written three articles for *Forbes*, including "Catch Me if you Can" which was widely lauded.
    8. John Grisham's first big book was *The Firm*. Then *The Pelican Brief* came shortly thereafter.
    9. My doctor, Dr. Cydes, recently wrote an article called "Genotyping for Asthma," which was published in the *Journal of the American Medical Association*.
    10. In the 1980s, *Cheers* was a huge hit on television. The episode called "One for the Road" is Norm's favorite.

3. Possessive Singular
    1. John's
    2. her brother's

3. friend's
4. teacher's
5. their friend Isis'
6. their brother's
7. one apple's
8. The institution's
9. one of the horse's
10. Central America's

4. Possessive Plural

1. The researchers'
2. the authors'
3. The Johnsons'
4. the children's
5. pies' crusts
6. quilts' colors
7. homes' roofs
8. my friends'
9. All three teachers'
10. Chemists'

4B. Correct the errors

1. All flight attendants'
2. The dog's
3. The cats' food bowls
4. team's
5. A baker's
6. Grace's
7. Smiths'
8. researchers'
9. no change
10. child's
11. children's
12. no change

13. writer's
14. no change
15. chef's
16. students'
17. no change
18. O'Malleys'
19. guitar's
20. friends'
21. birds'
22. no change
23. no change
24. student's
25. parents'

Quiz 1

1. Yasmine wanted to go to her friend Marc's house because he lived directly on hHermosa bBeach.
2. When Regan read the book tThe nNotebook for the first time, she was touched by the couple's love.
3. Terrence loves F. Scott Fitzgerald and was excited when DiCaprio played the main character in *The Great Gatsby*, as the actor's abilities are among the strongest of our time.
4. It was easy to hear the Johnsons' party from down the street. They hired a band called tThe aApex wWanderers, and when they broke into a cover of "dDon't sStop bBelievin'", you should've seen the street wake up and come out to sing in their pajamas.
5. Ted's sister Rebecca's best friend Susie has a dog named sSpike who loves to chew on Susie's shoes.
6. Melise could not be happier for the Gronsons, who got married over the weekend and are honeymooning in cCancun with their three dogs and their dogs' handlers.
7. The tLos aAngeles tTimes reported that the chapter "The fForest aAgain" in *Harry Potter and the dDeathly hHallows* is most people's favorite chapter, including Rowling's.
8. The couple's dog is usually pretty friendly.

9. When the white whale unexpectedly breached near the shore, people's coats got wet.
10. Josie's cat had kittens and now there are so many of them, her cats' purring can practically be heard from the neighbor's house.

5. Commas and Semicolons in a List

1. Peace, faith, and hope
2. Yes, no, or maybe
3. Margherite wrote the music, wrote the lyrics, recorded it, and played it live for us last weekend.
4. Raven, Musk and Company
5. The kids like mac and cheese, hot dogs, tater tots, etc.
6. When you want to take a hike, go on a cruise, or explore the coastline, Expert Adventures can help.
7. Like most people, she wakes up, takes a shower, and gets ready for the day, then leaves the house, fights commuter traffic, and gets to work just in time.
8. People with a lot of piercings in their lips, eyebrows, noses, etc. are interesting to look at and consider how those piercings affect their lives.
9. When I was little, I wanted to work at a big company like Corso, Bloomfield and Company, but as I grew older, I prefer to stay in smaller organizations where it's cozier, friendlier, and easier to get around.
10. Whether ocean water, tears, or sweat, salt water heals.

B. Punctuate the following sentences properly.

1. Josie's favorite movies are *Jaws; Gone in 60 Seconds* because of Nicholas Cage; and *The Godfather*, which was directed by Nicholas Cage's uncle.
2. Mario's favorite movies are *Casablanca, Ghost,* and *The Godfather*.
3. Hector loves talking about beaches; hot springs, which he goes to whenever he can; and disco music.
4. Linda's favorite subjects are travel, astronomy, and films from the 1940s.
5. Technology has made our lives both better in some ways and not as great in others. (no change)
6. When Elena asks you to go shopping with her, she'll ask you to help her pick everything out, hold her things, and get different sizes while she's in the dressing room.

7. Family relationships can be strong; beautiful, unless there are serious family problems; and also quite tough.
8. Rick's favorite hangout spots are race tracks and pool halls because he can make money in both. (no change)
9. People on vacation often don't pay attention to their things because they're looking around too much, spend a lot of money, and are sometimes at risk.
10. Julia couldn't handle oysters, which give us pearls by the way; octopus; or lobster because it looks like a giant insect.
11. When you go hiking in the jungle, be sure to bring a good reef-safe sunscreen, strong natural insect repellent made with peppermint or cinnamon, and a light broad-brimmed hat.
12. For a lot of people, television is a way of life, the commute is longer than it ought to be, and work is exhausting.

6. Appositives

1. Julia's teacher, the one with the white Cadillac, gave her a delicious cookie today.
2. My middle name, if you must know, is Herman.
3. The person who has the highest score will win the prize. (no change)
4. If you want to read a good book, legal thrillers, particularly those by Grisham, are my favorites.
5. When ships leave the harbor, even the little ones, they make a big wake behind them.
6. The woman standing over where the cookies are is my husband's boss. (no change)
7. Bavaria, where the Oktoberfest is held, gets a lot of snow in winter.
8. We didn't really want to go to the lake, the movies, or dinner, etc., this evening. (no change)
9. He saw us coming, but because he didn't know who we were, he did not take notice.
10. He'd better start talking, unless he's going to just shoot me, to get himself out of this jam.
11. My car, a red Honda Civic with 150,000 miles on it, needs new tires.
12. The insect, a long-legged spider that freaked me out whenever I saw it, dangled from the ceiling.
13. Julia's dress, a flowing silk gown with a silvery color, shimmered under the lights.
14. His favorite dessert, chocolate lava cake, was served last.
15. Jupiter has many moons none of which have rings.
16. That red bird, a huge and colorful toucan, is native to South America.

17. The building, an old factory in the newly renovated industrial district, was converted into apartments.
18. Grisham's latest novel, a thrilling legal mystery and absolute page-turner, kept me up all night.
19. Our neighbor, Mr. Thompson, owns the bakery downtown.
20. My dog, a youthful and playful golden retriever, loves fetch.
21. The president, a gifted orator and seasoned diplomat, gave a strong speech.
22. The puppy, a wriggling ball of grey and black fur, nipped my finger.
23. Picasso was one of the artists who changed modern art forever.
24. Her son, a college freshman, just moved into the dorms.
25. That bird, a colorful toucan, is native to South America.
26. Their dog scared away the burglars.
27. The artist, a master of watercolor, showcased his work.
28. Her new book, a psychological thriller, topped the charts.
29. My uncle who lives with us tells incredible bedtime stories.
30. Her painting was a vivid landscape, and it won first prize.
31. My phone which has a cracked screen still works fine.
32. The gem was a radiant sapphire, and it was priceless.
33. Her ring which was a precious family heirloom was stolen in the heist.
34. Our guide Fritz, a local historian, explained the ruins.
35. The astronaut, a veteran of three missions, spoke at the school.
36. The museum's highlight, a Van Gogh original, drew large crowds.
37. My professor was a Nobel laureate, and he gave an excellent lecture.
38. The bakery's specialty, blueberry muffins, sells out daily
39. My brother plays in a local band called Wags.
40. My mentor, a respected scientist, encouraged creativity.

7. Its/it's; Whose/who's

1. Who's calling this late at night, and whose phone keeps buzzing?
2. I don't know who's more excited for the trip, but whose idea was it originally?
3. She's the one who's always prepared, unlike the others whose materials are never ready.
4. Who's at the door, and whose keys are on the welcome mat?
5. That's the coach who's trained national champions—do you know whose team he's coaching now?

6. Who's been spreading that rumor, and whose story are we supposed to believe?
7. The company changed its logo again, and it's not an improvement.
8. That team knows its strengths, and it's using them well.
9. The cat licks its paws after it's had a messy meal.
10. The tree lost its leaves early this year, and it's probably due to the drought.
11. Every robot has its own programming, but it's still learning new tasks.

8. Hyphenation & Modifier Construction

1. The old-fashioned stove still works perfectly.
2. Elizabeth gave me a cold-hearted reply and walked away.
3. We booked a five-star restaurant for the celebration.
4. The Cossicks live in a family-friendly neighborhood.
5. Maribel's bright-eyed optimism inspired the team.
6. George is a soft-spoken man but carries great influence.
7. The hike was a once-in-a-lifetime experience.
8. Nancy is reading a coming-of-age novel.
9. Baxter was an open-minded student and welcomed new perspectives.
10. It's a last-minute decision, but we're going for it.
11. The 6-year-old child gave a heart-warming speech at the event.
12. Unbelievably, Henry had a four-inch pinky.

Exercise B

Correct the errors in the following sentences. Sometimes 1 word needs to be divided into 2, and sometimes 2 words need to be combined into one.

1. Tony's breakdown report explained everything clearly.
2. Tony hopes his car doesn't break down.
3. The printout is on the boss's desk because he doesn't like to print out things himself.
4. The handoff procedure needs to be reviewed because we're not sure it's safe to hand off like that.
5. Jack took his friends through the rundown part of town.
6. Jerry had to run down the information he was after.
7. Mick went in for a checkup.
8. The doctor likes to check up on her patients regularly.

9. Tabitha meditates every day.
10. Oscar's everyday meditation starts with yoga.
11. You have to log in before you can proceed with registration.
12. They will keep your login information for next time.

Quiz 2

1. The committee includes Dr. Harris, the dean of students; Ms. Lopez, the financial officer; and Mr. Grant, head of campus security.
2. This is the company who*se* materials are always well-done.
3. It was a last-minute decision that changed everything.
4. For dinner we had a very delicious and well-seasoned lentil loaf, mashed potatoes made with plant milks and butters, green beans, and apple pie. (no change)
5. It*'s* an important report so I hope it*'s* no problem to complete it on time.
6. Johanna, the twenty-five-year-old teacher, just got promoted.
7. Julia's teacher, the one with the white Cadillac, gave her a delicious cookie today.
8. The Eiffel Tower attracts millions of tourists yearly and is the reason so many tourism businesses in the area do so well. (no change)
9. Who*'s* driving your car, and who*se* car is this?
10. The museum features works by Monet; O'Keeffe; and Hokusai, the Japanese printmaker. (no change)
11. The team knows it*s* strengths even if it*s* top player is injured and they know it*'s* all going to be fine.
12. My middle name, if you must know, is Herman.
13. The man who*se* wife is speaking is my professor.
14. Professor Jayne, who*se* wife is speaking, is my professor.
15. I need to finish the budget report, respond to client emails, organize the files, and call the printer. (no change)
16. This is a user-friendly interface.
17. Please wake up the gardener; he's asleep in the shade again.
18. I don't procrastinate because I don't like to play catchup.
19. The dog that barked all night and prevented any of us from getting any sleep belongs to my neighbor to the left. (no change)
20. That dog, even though he may be annoying, keeps the neighborhood safe.

9. Parallel Structure

1. They practiced piano together, played ~~ing~~ their best duets and listened ~~ing~~ to the rain.
2. The boys rode bikes through the park, raced each other and enjoyed ~~ing~~ the cool afternoon.
3. The fruit is ripe, ~~it is~~ fresh, and delicious.
4. I like him not for who he may be, but for who he is now.
5. The cows liked standing in the pasture, enjoying the day, and chewing ~~ed~~ their cud.
6. It's not that she doesn't like it; it's that she can't stand it.
7. She baked cookies, decorated ~~ing~~ them and handed ~~ing~~ them out.
8. Ilena knew that she was running late, ~~that~~ her boss would be angry, and she would get written up.
9. We arrived at the party, brought ~~bringing~~ a gift and were surprised to see the party already in full swing.
10. She loves swimming in the ocean, feeling the sand between her toes and watching the sunset. (no change)

10. Be Consistent

Streamline the following paragraphs.

a. Last summer I went on a road trip with my friends to the coast. We were all so excited because we had been planning this trip for months. As we drove along the scenic highway, we reminisced about all the adventures we had already experienced together. The scenery was breathtaking and we couldn't wait to explore the beach once we arrived.

b. When I was younger, I used to spend summers at my grandparents' farm. The memories of those days are still vivid in my mind. We would wake up early every morning to feed the chickens and gather eggs. The sun would be shining brightly as we worked in the fields, planting vegetables and tending to the crops. Those summers taught me the value of hard work and the beauty of living close to nature.

c. As a child, I often spent hours exploring the woods near my grandmother's house. The trees towered over me, casting dappled shadows on the forest floor. I would climb trees and build forts from fallen branches, imagining myself as an explorer in a vast wilderness. Now, whenever I visit, the familiar paths and secret hideaways still evoke a sense of adventure and nostalgia.

d. Last night, my friends and I decided to go out for dinner at our favorite restaurant in town. As we walked in, the familiar aroma of grilled steaks and garlic butter filled the air, instantly transporting me back to all the previous memorable meals we've had here. We ordered our usual dishes and caught up on each other's lives, laughing and reminiscing about old times. Now, as I reflect on that night out, I realize how much those moments of camaraderie mean to me, both then and now.

e. In my high school classroom, the walls are adorned with colorful posters and educational charts. The desks are arranged in neat rows, reminiscent of how they used to be when I sat among my classmates, eagerly absorbing lessons. Today, the teacher stands at the whiteboard, explaining complex math problems with the same patience and clarity that I remember from my time as a student. As I observe the students diligently taking notes and raising their hands to ask questions, I remember my own journey through this classroom, where learning has always been a blend of challenge and discovery.

f. In the heart of the dense jungle, ancient trees tower over the lush undergrowth, their canopies providing shelter to myriad creatures as they did for centuries. Monkeys swing effortlessly from branch to branch, their calls echoing through the verdant canopy just as they have for generations. The air is thick with humidity, carrying scents of rich earth and exotic blooms that have attracted explorers and researchers alike for centuries. As I trek deeper into this wilderness, I am struck by how the jungle preserves its timeless allure, captivating visitors with its untamed beauty and unending mysteries.

11. Sentence Grammar

In each of the following sentences, underline the primary components of each sentence: the main subject, main verb, and main object, if any. Remember that subjects and objects are always nouns.

1. The small <u>boy</u> with the soccer-star father <u>kicked</u> <u>the ball</u> over the fence and through the window of the neighbors' house, causing a great ruckus and a few hundred dollars in damage.

2. <u>Gertrude</u>, a friend of my aunt over in Helmsdale, east of the highway, <u>called</u> today absolutely out of the blue for no reason at all but just to say hello.
3. During the cold winter months, the old <u>woman</u> with the bright red scarf <u>walked</u> slowly and carefully down the icy sidewalk to the small corner store at the end of the block.
4. Beneath the pale blue sky dotted with wispy clouds, the <u>kite</u> with the long green tail <u>fluttered</u> wildly in the strong gusts of wind blowing in from the coast.
5. The <u>man</u> with the long gray beard, sun-damaged skin, and weathered backpack <u>wandered</u> <u>the streets</u> of the city looking for a safe place to rest.
6. In the shadow of the mountain, the <u>village</u> with cobblestone streets, colorful shutters, and hand-painted signs <u>welcomed</u> weary <u>travelers</u> with the inviting aromas of fresh bread and blooming jasmine.
7. The crowded <u>train</u> with flickering lights, sticky floors, and a constant screeching sound <u>shuddered and groaned</u> its way through the underground tunnel toward the city center.
8. The aging, agile <u>chef</u> with tattoos on his arms, a towel over his shoulder, and sweat on his brow <u>chopped</u> vegetables at lightning speed while shouting instructions across the noisy kitchen.
9. The enormous oak <u>tree</u> with twisted limbs, thick bark, and a hollow trunk full of squirrels <u>stood</u> firmly in the middle of the park as children ran in circles around its base.
10. After months of training and preparation, the young <u>athlete</u> with a determined expression and a powerful stride <u>sprinted</u> across the finish line under the blazing afternoon sun.

12. Comma Before the Main Clause

1. After the storm ended, the sun broke through the clouds.
2. Despite her fear of heights, she climbed the tall rock wall.
3. To finish the project on time, we worked late into the night.
4. With tears in his eyes, he handed her the letter.
5. While the others were sleeping, the dog kept watch by the door.
6. Having forgotten his umbrella, he arrived soaking wet.
7. Before the movie began, the theater dimmed its lights.
8. Covered in flour from baking, the child smiled proudly at the frog.
9. Although he was exhausted, he continued hiking up the trail.
10. Frustrated by the delay, the passengers demanded answers.

11. In order to understand the concept, you must read the chapter carefully.
12. Just as the sun began to rise, the birds started singing.

13. Joining Clauses

1. The boy went to school, but the girl stayed home.
2. You can come if you want, or you can stay home if you prefer.
3. She says she doesn't eat dairy, yet I see her with an ice cream cone every day.
4. Cheese and crackers go well together, so let's buy some cheese and crackers.
5. I forgive you for yelling at me, for I know you do not fully understand.
6. We wouldn't want that to happen, nor would you want it to happen, either.
7. The children and their parents are all invited to the program, but many of them live too far away to attend.
8. I got to choose our vacation spot this year, so I picked the Maldives.
9. The weather up north is very cold in winter, yet many men wear sandals.
10. Dogs often bark a lot, but they rarely bite.

B.

1. I love horses; he likes turtles.
   I love horses. He likes turtles.
2. I went down to the store; I didn't know what I was going to buy.
   I went down to the store. I didn't know what I was going to buy.
3. When we grow up, I want to study geology, and my sister wants to study history.
4. The fan over the porch swing wasn't working; neither was the fan in the kitchen.
   The fan over the porch swing wasn't working. Neither was the fan in the kitchen.
5. Tomatoes are pretty easy to grow, but watermelons are a different story.
6. I didn't love the house; something told me to rent it.
   I didn't love the house. Something told me to rent it.
7. We're nearly finished with this section; then we can move on to the next one.
   We're nearly finished with this section. Then we can move on to the next one.
8. I love going to the zoo, but I don't love the smell of the cages. (no change)
9. Families sometimes fight, but I love mine more than anything.
10. Calculus isn't the easiest for most people, yet some people pick it up very easily.

14. Run-ons and Fragments

(punctuation may vary between [;], [.], or [, + conjunction])

1. The sun came out, so we went to the beach.
2. He's allergic to cats, yet he owns three of them.
3. I need to finish my homework; I also have to clean my room.
4. The dog barked. The neighbors complained.
5. He's very talented, but he doesn't practice much.
6. I love reading mystery novels; I don't enjoy horror.
7. She smiled, and he looked away.
8. It's raining outside. I forgot my umbrella.
9. We met at the café, and we stayed for hours.
10. I like hiking. I don't like camping.

B. Fragments (underlines)

1. <u>After the long drive through the mountains and across the valley.</u>
2. The lights flickered, but the power stayed on.
3. <u>Despite the rain, the wind, and the cold that chilled them to the bone.</u>
4. She smiled and waved as the train pulled away.
5. He carefully packed the fragile dishes into a box labeled "kitchen."
6. <u>While running late for the meeting and juggling three phone calls at once.</u>
7. The dog barked wildly when the mailman approached the gate.
8. <u>Even though the deadline was approaching and the team hadn't started.</u>
9. They finished the project ahead of schedule and under budget.
10. <u>If you're ever near the old mill by the river at sunset.</u>

15. Keep Related Words Together

Correct the errors in the following sentences.

1. He went down the beach that was so great for beachcombing and looked at the surf.
2. She watched the beautiful sunset that she liked so much with a hint of sadness.
3. Underneath the old bridge where my parents lived, the river flowed quietly.
4. During the cold winter nights that lasted for three long months, they gathered around the fireplace.
5. With a gentle touch that was characteristic of her family's touch, she comforted the crying child.

6. Near the edge of the cliff where I fell one time, wildflowers bloomed beautifully as if to mark my spot.
7. Over the course of many years hiding in his art studio, he mastered the art of painting and made a splash in the art world upon his debut.
8. Despite all odds that were against them, they completed the difficult tasks.
9. With a knife that he kept razor sharp, he cut the tomatoes.
10. Unless my memory fails me, which happens more often than I'd like to admit, I think I know you from somewhere.

16. Don't Dangle the Modifier

1. From too much exercise at the gym, my muscles ached with each movement.
2. Building a sandcastle, I noticed the tide began to rise.
3. Cooking dinner, she noticed the aroma filled the kitchen.
4. For hiking in the woods, the trail markers were unclear.
5. Speaking with a friend, I was surprised that the conversation took an unexpected turn.
6. Eating breakfast, I was annoyed that the phone rang incessantly.
7. As I was listening to music, my thoughts drifted away.
8. Typing on the keyboard, I found the letters seemed to blur together.
9. Playing with the dog, I was surprised when the leash suddenly broke.
10. Running to catch the bus, I nearly lost my bag as it slipped from my shoulder.

Grammar Exam

1. Derek loved the short story "The Lottery," found in his recent published collection *What Makes Me Tick*.
2. The sSun aAlso rRises is one of Hemingway's classic novels.
3. Joey had one dog. The dog's collars were a range of colors.
4. The teachers' lounge had a pinball machine.
5. Bettina packed a rechargeable flashlight, sleeping bag, and water-safe matches.
6. Roger's dog, a golden retriever, loves to swim in the Amazon River even though it's terribly muddy.
7. Who's going to lead the meeting today?
8. Lori said she wanted to go, but leaping from a fast-moving train wasn't her best option.

9. "Please, everyone fill out the signup sheet so you can sign up for our newsletter."
10. The tourists loved to hike, swim, and surf.
11. After the meeting, we went to lunch.
12. Still hungry after lunch, the firemen jumped into the cold lake.
13. We left early; it was raining.
14. For example, the one on the left is mine.
15. While I was typing on the laptop, the cat jumped on the keys.

17. *Be* Verbs

1. The knowledgeable teacher taught the lesson.
2. The delicious and moist cake tasted delicious.
3. Blooming flowers fill our garden.
4. She parked the car in the driveway.
5. The new playground excites the kids.
6. He sent the email to all employees.
7. She didn't want to be happy; she preferred sadness.
8. She cleaned her room every morning.
9. He watered his flowers daily.
10. People know her for her kindness.

18. Avoid Negation

1. The weather is bad today.
2. That test was easier than I thought it would be.
3. The train is running late.
4. The meeting had some surprises.
5. She disagreed with the decision.
6. The cookies are raw.
7. His phone is broken.
8. He's unprepared for the presentation.
9. I am uninterested in that book.
10. The dog is friendly with strangers.

19. Delete Unnecessary Words

1. ~~In order~~ to sell the cookies, we have to bake them first.
2. ~~There are~~ a lot of white cars are in the parking lot.
3. ~~There is~~ a strange noise is coming from the attic.
4. The package ~~that~~ I ordered has not ~~yet~~ arrived, ~~which is~~ surprising ~~to me~~ because it was supposed to be delivered yesterday.
5. She isn't feeling well today, unfortunately, ~~which means~~ so she will have to work extra hard when she comes back ~~to make up for lost time~~.
6. The project ~~that~~ we have all been working really hard on ~~for the past few weeks~~ is not due until next week, ~~which is~~ a huge relief for everyone ~~involved~~.
7. The store ~~which is~~ conveniently located on Main Street is not open on Sundays ~~at all~~, ~~despite the fact that~~ even though many people might want to shop then~~on that day of the week~~.
8. He really does not like to eat spicy food at all, especially during any of his meals, whether that be breakfast, lunch, or dinner, as it tends to upset his stomach and cause discomfort.
9. The dog ~~that lives~~ next door simply does not bark at ~~any~~ strangers ~~in the neighborhood~~, ~~which is rather~~ unusual for a dog of that breed, ~~as they are~~ known for being protective and alert.
10. ~~There are~~ many beautiful flowers are in the garden this spring.
11. For ~~the purpose of~~ clarity, please be succinct.

Quiz 3

be, negation, excess words

1. He ~~did not~~ failed to understand that question on the test.
2. The presentation ~~was~~ came across as boring and poorly organized.
3. He ~~is afraid of~~ fears failure.
4. He returned ~~back~~ to the office after lunch.
5. She ~~made the decision to~~ postponed the meeting.
6. It's ~~not unusual~~ common to feel nervous before a big event.
7. They were not impressed disappointed by the presentation. The presentation disappointed them.
8. The team's ~~was~~ successful ~~because they were efficient~~ stemmed from their efficiency.

9. ~~At this point in time,~~ we need to focus our attention on results.
10. ~~Due to the fact that it was raining,~~ we canceled the event because of rain.

20. Paragraph Cohesiveness

1. *Saving Grain* is set on a farm outside of a small town in central Missouri. The land is 100 acres and primarily used for oat and wheat production. At the barn, there are two silos, one for each grain type. ~~Brian is the farmer and Melissa is the farmer's wife. They have three children.~~ The land had been passed down in the family for a few generations and has always been farmland because the soil is so rich.

2. The protests of the 1960s that were centered around the University of California, Berkeley comprised significant elements of greater social movements that characterized the era. The protests centered around the university played a pivotal role in the broader context of anti-war activism, civil rights, and the free speech movement. ~~As the conflict in Vietnam escalated, the anti-war movement grew in size and influence.~~ The Berkeley protests were often led by students, although many non-students were also involved.

3. The movie industry has evolved over time. Currently, the rise of streaming platforms has altered how audiences consume movies, in turn challenging the entire movie distribution models and the dominance of theater releases. With the proliferation of streaming services, audiences can now access a vast library of films from around the world, anytime and anywhere. ~~From IMAX and 3D screenings to independent films and their intimate storytelling, the movie theater remains a cultural institution that continues to adapt and evolve with the changing preferences of its audiences.~~ The dramatic shift toward streaming has raised questions about the role of cinema and theaters as we move into the future.

21. Paragraph Structure

1. <u>Many species of frogs in the Amazon produce powerful toxins through secretions in their skin.</u> These toxins are the frogs' defense mechanisms against predators. The level of toxicity of their secretions varies among frog species, with some highly lethal to predators and others much less potent. The poison dart frogs, known for their stunning colors and powerful toxins, are one such frog. Native to Central and South America, the poison dart frogs are some of the most toxic animals on Earth,

with some species having enough toxicity to kill a human. <u>The animal's skin secretions keep it safe from predators in the jungle.</u>

2. <u>The largest planet in our solar system, Jupiter is a majestic gas giant.</u> Its awe-inspiring, swirling storms and fascinating moons captivate astronomers and enthusiasts alike. Jupiter dominates the solar system with a diameter of more than 11 times that of earth and a mass of more than 300 times greater. Behind clouds that cover its surface, Jupiter's atmosphere consists of turbulent winds, thunderstorms, and the Great Red Spot, a storm that has raged for centuries. <u>Its massive size and powerful storms make Jupiter a source of wonder and curiosity.</u>

Correct the errors in the topic and/or concluding sentences in the paragraphs below.

3. When tectonic plates beneath the earth's surface shift and release energy, the movement sends shockwaves rippling through the earth's crust. When these tectonic plates move along fault lines, where stress builds up until it is released in the form of a seismic wave, this is what we know as an earthquake. An earthquake's intensity is measured on the Richter scale. Although earthquakes all have an epicenter, their effects can be felt hundreds or even thousands of kilometers away. In urban areas with dense populations, the impact of earthquakes can be devastating. <u>The shifting of these tectonic plates and their resulting earthquakes occur without warning.</u>
(no concluding sentence.)

4. <u>Bridges are tremendous feats of engineering.</u> The process of bridge building begins with site surveys and geological assessments, necessary to ascertain the bridge's optimal location. Topography, soil composition, hydrology, and environmental impact must all be considered to ensure the bridge can withstand the forces of nature and provide safe passage for those who want to use it. ~~The next step is to design the bridge structure.~~ <u>When building a bridge, many elements require careful attention.</u>
(no topic sentence. The paragraph begins with too much detail. The concluding sentence is not appropriate as it introduces the next topic rather than concluding this topic.)

5. Ethereal beings of folklore, forest fairies are said to live in the hidden realms of wooded areas, where they dance under the sunlight and whisper secrets to the trees. They are often depicted as small and graceful, with delicate shimmering wings.

Legend has it that forest fairies are the guardians of nature, protecting the forest's flora and fauna and helping maintain the delicate ecosystem balance. Some say they possess magical powers: They can influence plant growth, soothe wounded animals, and enchant travelers who venture too close to their homes. ~~In Celtic folklore, they are known as "sidhe" or "fae".~~ <u>Forest fairies bring a delightful presence to the woods.</u>

(Concluding sentence is inappropriate. It introduces a different topic. There is no actual concluding sentence in this paragraph.)

22.   Transitions

To set up an Instagram account, start by downloading the app from the App Store or Google Play. **Next**, open the app and tap "Sign Up" to create a new account using your email or phone number. **Then**, choose a username that represents you or your brand and create a strong password. **After that**, you'll be prompted to add a profile photo, a short bio, and optional links to your website or other social profiles. **Once everything is filled out**, tap "Done" to complete the setup. **Finally**, begin exploring Instagram by following friends, choosing interests, and sharing your first post.

Climate change matters for many urgent reasons. **First of all**, it threatens the stability of ecosystems that support life on Earth. **In addition**, rising temperatures increase the frequency of extreme weather events, such as hurricanes and droughts. **As a result**, communities face greater risks to their safety, health, and food supply. **Furthermore**, climate change contributes to rising sea levels, which endanger coastal cities around the world. **Not only that**, but it also affects global economies by damaging infrastructure and disrupting agriculture. **On top of everything else**, the most vulnerable populations suffer the greatest impacts. **Therefore**, taking action now is essential for the future of the planet's ability to sustain human life.

Quiz 4

(topic and concluding sentences, cohesion/relevance, and transitions)

Learning how to surf is a rewarding challenge that offers both physical and mental benefits. **To begin with**, surfing is an excellent full-body workout that builds strength, balance, and endurance. **Moreover**, it provides a unique connection to nature, allowing you to spend time outdoors and develop respect for the ocean. **In addition**, surfing teaches patience and resilience, as progress comes through consistent practice and overcoming frustration. ~~You can learn to surf at any age.~~ **As you improve**, you'll gain confidence, not just in your athletic abilities but also in your ability to face new challenges. **Beyond the personal growth**, surfing can be a great way to meet new people and join a supportive, adventurous community. **All things considered**, learning to surf is not only fun but also an empowering way to grow stronger, calmer, and more connected.

- Missing topic sentence
- One irrelevant sentence (you can learn to surf at any age)
- Poor concluding sentence
- No transitions present

23. First Words Matter

A. Underline the theme in each sentence.

1. We <u>walked</u> along the quiet beach at sunset.
2. She <u>carried</u> a basket full of ripe oranges.
3. The <u>road</u> through the mountains was narrow and winding.
4. We didn't understand the <u>strange</u> noise coming from the attic. (many words before it)
5. He <u>chose</u> to paint his room a soft green.
6. I <u>forgot</u> my umbrella, so I got soaked.
7. The <u>teacher</u> gave me my A paper.
8. The <u>cake</u> smelled delicious as it came out of the oven.
9. He <u>opened</u> the letter and a smile stretched across his face.
10. With no <u>warning</u>, the fire alarm started blaring.

B. Rewrite each sentence with intentional placement in the theme position.

1. At sunset, we walked along the quiet beach.
2. Ripe oranges filling her basket, she carried it home.
3. The mountain road was narrow and winding.
4. The strange noise coming from the attic confused us.
5. A soft-green paintbrush in hand, he painted his room.

6. My umbrella left at home, I got soaked.
7. The A paper made me smile as the teacher returned it to me.
8. The aroma of chocolate cake filled the air as it came out of the oven.
9. A smile stretched across his face as he opened the letter.
10. The fire alarm started blaring with no warning.

24. The End-Weight Principle

1. They stepped outside and there, dancing in the street, they were greeted by a surprise flash mob.
2. He opened the umbrella and inside, tucked into the handle, he found a love note.
3. He opened the old trunk and, hidden inside, he discovered a collection of rare coins.
4. She picked up the phone and on the other end she heard her favorite song.
5. As they walked along the beach, they found, washed ashore, a message in a bottle.
6. The children gathered around as the magician reached into his hat and pulled out a rabbit.
7. Fireworks suddenly lit up the night sky as the clock struck midnight.
8. Opening the closet door, she found, tied with a ribbon, a stack of love letters.
9. He dove into the lake and emerged with a pearl necklace.
10. He pulled out a camera and captured a surprise proposal.

25. Prepositional Phrases are Mobile Modifiers

Identification and placement

A. Underline all prepositional phrases
1. After a long day at work, with her bag slung over her shoulder and her phone buzzing in her pocket, she finally walked into the quiet comfort of her home.
2. In the middle of the night, under a sky full of stars, the astronomer adjusted his telescope with care and precision.
3. <u>Behind the counter</u>, <u>next to the cash register</u>, a small handwritten sign reminded customers to support local businesses <u>during the holidays</u>.
4. Across the river and through the fields of tall grass, the children chased fireflies with laughter echoing in the warm summer air.

5. On the edge of the forest, beneath a canopy of ancient trees, the hikers set up their campsite for the night.

B. Move the prepositional phrases to all reasonable locations. Note: not all options are presented here because there are a lot of options for each sentence. These answers are some of them, but you may have different options.

1. After a long day at work, with her bag slung over her shoulder and her phone buzzing in her pocket, she finally walked into the quiet comfort of her home.
    a. She finally walked into the quiet comfort of her home after a long day at work, with her bag slung over her shoulder and her phone buzzing in her pocket.
    b. She, after a long day at work, finally walked into the quiet comfort of her home with her bag slung over her shoulder and her phone buzzing in her pocket.
    c. With her bag slung over her shoulder, she finally walked, after a long day at work, into the quiet comfort of her home with her phone buzzing in her pocket.
    d. She finally walked into the quiet comfort of her home with her bag slung over her shoulder, her phone buzzing in her pocket, after a long day at work.
2. In the middle of the night, under a sky full of stars, the astronomer adjusted his telescope with care and precision.
    a. Under a sky full of stars, the astronomer, in the middle of the night, adjusted his telescope with care and precision.
    b. With care and precision, the astronomer adjusted his telescope in the middle of the night under a sky full of stars.
    c. The astronomer adjusted his telescope in the middle of the night, under a sky full of stars, with care and precision.
    d. The astronomer adjusted his telescope with care and precision in the middle of the night under a sky full of stars.
3. Behind the counter, next to the cash register, a small handwritten sign reminded customers to support local businesses during the holidays.
    a. Behind the counter, a small handwritten sign next to the cash register reminded customers to support local businesses during the holidays.

b. A small handwritten sign behind the counter, next to the cash register, reminded customers to support local businesses during the holidays.
   c. Next to the cash register behind the counter, a small handwritten sign reminded customers to support local businesses during the holidays.
   d. During the holidays, a small handwritten sign behind the counter and next to the cash register reminded customers to support local businesses.
4. Across the river and through the fields of tall grass, the children chased fireflies with laughter echoing in the warm summer air.
   a. The children chased fireflies in the warm summer air with laughter echoing across the river and through the fields of tall grass. (changes meaning)
   b. With laughter echoing in the warm summer air, the children chased fireflies across the river and through the fields of tall grass.
   c. The children chased fireflies across the river and through the fields of tall grass, with laughter echoing in the warm summer air.
   d. The children, with laughter echoing in the warm summer air, chased fireflies through the fields of tall grass and across the river.
5. On the edge of the forest, beneath a canopy of ancient trees, the hikers set up their campsite for the night.
   a. On the edge of the forest, the hikers set up their campsite for the night beneath a canopy of ancient trees.
   b. The hikers, on the edge of the forest, set up their campsite for the night beneath a canopy of ancient trees.
   c. Beneath a canopy of ancient trees on the edge of the forest, the hikers set up their campsite for the night.
   d. The hikers set up their campsite for the night on the edge of the forest beneath a canopy of ancient trees.

Prepositional phrases

Reduction: exercise C

1. After a long day at work, with her bag slung over her shoulder and her phone buzzing in her pocket, she finally walked into the quiet comfort of her home.
   a. She finally walked into the quiet, end-of-day comfort of her home, her shoulder-slung bag bouncing as her pocket-buzzing phone vibrated.

b. She finally walked into the quiet, post-work comfort of her home, her over-the-shoulder bag shifting slightly as her pocket-vibrating phone hummed.
   c. Carrying a shoulder-slung bag and a pocket-buzzing phone, she finally walked into the peaceful, after-work comfort of her home.
2. In the middle of the night, under a sky full of stars, the astronomer adjusted his telescope with care and precision.
   a. The astronomer adjusted his telescope with careful precision in the quiet middle-of-the-night darkness.
   b. Under a star-filled sky, the late-night astronomer adjusted his telescope with steady precision.
   c. The astronomer adjusted his telescope with midnight care beneath a star-splashed sky.
3. Behind the counter, next to the cash register, a small handwritten sign reminded customers to support local businesses during the holidays.
   a. A small handwritten, counter-side sign reminded customers to support local businesses during the holidays.
   b. A cash-register-side sign, handwritten and small, reminded customers to support local businesses during the holidays.
   c. A small handwritten sign near the register and behind the counter reminded customers to support local businesses during the holidays.
4. Across the river and through the fields of tall grass, the children chased fireflies with laughter echoing in the warm summer air.
   a. The children chased fireflies in the warm summer air, running through tall-grass fields and crossing the wide river.
   b. The firefly-chasing children ran across the river and through the tall-grass fields, laughter echoing in the summer air.
   c. The children chased fireflies, laughing through tall-grass fields and across the wide river in the warm summer air.
5. On the edge of the forest, beneath a canopy of ancient trees, the hikers set up their campsite for the night.
   a. The forest-edge hikers set up their campsite beneath an ancient-tree canopy for the night.
   b. Beneath an ancient-tree canopy, the hikers set up their forest-edge campsite for the night.
   c. The hikers set up a night campsite under an ancient-tree canopy at the forest edge.

26. Vary Sentences

A. The sun was shining, and the birds were singing happily in the park. Children's ~~were playing in the park, and their~~ laughter wafted through the air. When the ice cream truck arrived at the park, ~~so~~ the kids lined up to get a cool treat. Dogs were chasing after balls, and kids were chasing the dogs. ~~The day was wonderful, and~~ everyone enjoyed the warm, sunny weather on this wonderful day.

B. ~~Although the sun was shining,~~ the sunny day was made pleasant by a cool breeze. As children played in the park, parents watched them from nearby benches. ~~When the ice cream truck arrived,~~ the kids lined up eagerly when the ice-cream truck arrived. ~~While~~ everyone enjoyed their treats, and sounds of laughter filled the air. ~~Since it was such a perfect day,~~ everyone stayed outside until sunset on such a perfect day.

C. In the heart of the city, amid tall skyscrapers and busy crowds, lies a quiet park. ~~Inside that park,~~ under the shade of old trees, sits an old stone fountain. ~~Around the fountain, on benches worn smooth,~~ people gather around the fountain ~~to rest and chat~~ on benches worn smooth to rest and chat. A picture of a famous poet stands near the park entrance, beside a flowerbed in bloom. ~~stands a picture of a famous poet~~. On the other side of the statue, along the path, visitors stroll and enjoy the peace.

27. Quantity as a Rhetorical Tool

Fruit plays a vital role in a balanced diet for several key reasons. First, fruits are rich in essential vitamins and minerals, such as vitamin C, potassium, and fiber, which support body function and boost the immune system. These nutrients help the body fight infections, regulate blood pressure, and maintain digestive health. Second, fruits are naturally low in fat and calories, making them a smart choice for those aiming to manage or lose weight. They also provide a sweet and satisfying alternative to processed snacks and desserts. <u>Finally, many fruits contain powerful antioxidants that reduce inflammation and protect cells from damage. Regular consumption of antioxidant-rich fruits like berries and citrus may lower the risk of heart disease and certain cancers</u>. Fortunately, nature offers a wide variety of fruits so there's something for everyone to incorporate into their healthy diet.

28.   Strategic Word Choice

1. The sunrise blazed through the pines.
2. She slipped into the lounge and sank into a chair.
3. The breeze made the afternoon feel crisp and clean.
4. He grabbed his cell and fired off a quick call.
5. They strolled into the market to gather supplies.
6. A novel lay forgotten on the countertop.
7. We devoured dinner just after sunset.
8. He gazed out the window, watching the cars drift by.
9. She scribbled a thought into her sketchbook.
10. The discussion dragged on for nearly an hour.

Quiz 5

(answers will vary)

Original:

The boy sat on the porch. The dog lay at his feet. The sun shone through the trees. A breeze moved across the yard. The leaves rustled in the wind. Birds chirped from the branches above. A car passed on the road nearby. The boy listened to the sounds of the afternoon.

Rewrite option 1:

The boy rested on the porch, his dog at his feet. Rays of sunlight filtered through the trees. A breeze swept across the yard, rustling the leaves. Birds called from above and a car rolled past on the road. The boy absorbed the sounds of the afternoon.

Rewrite option 2:

On the porch, the boy rested, the dog at his feet. Sunlight broke through the trees. A breeze drifted over the yard, whispering the leaves in the wind. Birdsong filled the air and a car drove down the road. The afternoon sounds brought the boy sheer delight.

Rewrite option 3:

The boy lingered on the porch, the dog resting quietly beside him. Sunlight streamed through the trees, a gentle breeze floated across the yard, and leaves danced in the wind. Birds symphonized their melodies and a car passed on the road. The boy tuned into the afternoon delights.

Composition Quiz

Passage

The room was not very clean, and there was not much furniture in it. It was kind of small, but it was still comfortable enough for the guests to stay. There wasn't any obvious damage, but there were some minor scratches on the walls. The lighting was not very bright, which was not really a problem for most people. It was basically a simple room, but it was suitable for what was needed at the time.

Answers will vary. Note the variations in tone.

Rewrite 1

Josie's space was small but efficient. The room looked dirty and sparsely furnished. Small but workable, it welcomed guests easily. Minor scratches marked the walls, yet any real damage remained unseen. Soft lighting created a cozy atmosphere, pleasing most visitors. Simple in design, the room met every essential need.

Rewrite 2

His apartment fit his personality. Dingy and minimalistic, the room offered few seating options. A compact space, it provided guests with just enough comfort. Faintly scratched walls hid any real damage. Faint lighting brightened the space just enough. Basic but functional, the room served its purpose.

Rewrite 3

Tony agreed to host this week. His guests entered a less-than-clean, minimally furnished room. Compact yet cozy, it provided adequate comfort. Scratches appeared on the walls without revealing real damage. Soft lighting bathed the space, welcoming visitors warmly. Basic yet practical, the room fulfilled its intended role.

Grammar and Composition Exam

Johns favorite book, the catcher in the rye is a great read but it's not always easy to understand. the characters struggles, their emotions and the setting of the novel are what makes it so special; and its message is timeless. reading it slowly and carefully it helps to grasp the themes better and it will improve you're understanding. the book is one of the classics and its one that everyone should read.

Rewrite 1

John loves *The Catcher in the Rye*, a book that challenges readers and calls for careful attention. The novel's characters struggle deeply, and their emotional journeys coupled with the vivid setting create a memorable story; its timeless message resonant across generations. Slowly reading the book reveals its rich themes and enhances understanding. This classic novel remains essential reading for everyone.

Rewrite 2

The Catcher in the Rye ranks as John's favorite book because it offers a profound look at human struggles. The characters' intense emotions and the novel's detailed setting combine to create a special story; its message continues to inspire readers. Careful reading uncovers important themes and improves comprehension. Readers consider this classic a must-read.

Rewrite 3

John admires *The Catcher in the Rye* for its complexity and depth. Struggles faced by the characters, their raw emotions, and the evocative setting enrich the novel; its timeless message leaves a lasting impact. Reading the book attentively reveals deeper meanings and strengthens understanding. As a classic, it deserves a place on everyone's bookshelf.

Genres

(some answers will vary)

Academic Writing

Passage
Butterflies (Order Lepidoptera) are well-studied insects renowned for their complex life cycles and ecological significance. Beginning as eggs laid on specific host plants, their development progresses through distinct larval (caterpillar), pupal (chrysalis), and adult stages. This metamorphosis is a key adaptation allowing butterflies to exploit diverse ecological niches. As pollinators, butterflies play a vital role in plant reproduction by transferring pollen between flowers while feeding on nectar. Their sensitivity to environmental changes, including habitat loss and climate shifts, underscores their importance as bioindicators for monitoring ecosystem health and biodiversity trends.

Average Sentence Length
There are 5 sentences. Total word count is 85 words, so the average sentence length is 17 words per sentence.

Verbs	host plants	bioindicators
are	development	health
beginning	stages	trends
laid	metamorphosis	
progresses	adaptation	*Modifiers*
allowing	niches	well-studied
play	pollinators	complex
transferring	role	distinct
feeding	reproduction	larval
underscores	pollen	pupal
	flowers	adult
Nouns	nectar	key
Butterflies	sensitivity	diverse
insects	changes	ecological
life cycles	habitat loss	vital
significance	climate shifts	environmental
eggs	importance	

General Vocabulary
The vocabulary is technical and academic, focusing on scientific and ecological terms.

Unique Characteristics

This passage uses a formal and precise tone, typical of academic writing. It is informative and concise, providing clear explanations of scientific concepts.

Sentence Structure Characteristics

Structured and Precise: Clearly structured with specific scientific terms (e.g., "Butterflies (Order Lepidoptera) are well-studied insects...").

Technical Vocabulary: Uses domain-specific language (e.g., "metamorphosis," "bioindicators").

Objective Tone: Maintains an objective, factual tone throughout (e.g., "Their sensitivity to environmental changes...").

Analytical Writing

Passage

Butterflies serve as fascinating subjects for ecological analysis due to their pivotal role in pollination and their sensitivity to environmental changes. As pollinators, butterflies contribute to the reproduction of countless plant species, thereby supporting biodiversity and ecosystem stability. Their lifecycle, characterized by metamorphosis from egg to caterpillar to pupa and finally to adult butterfly, underscores their adaptability and resilience. Scientists study butterfly populations as indicators of environmental health, monitoring fluctuations in species diversity and abundance to assess the impacts of habitat loss, climate change, and pesticide use. Understanding these factors is crucial for implementing effective conservation strategies aimed at preserving butterfly populations and their invaluable ecosystem services.

Average Sentence Length

There are 5 sentences. Total word count is 104 words, so the average sentence length is about 20.8 words per sentence.

Verbs	analysis	scientists
serve	role	populations
contribute	pollination	indicators
supporting	changes	health
characterized	pollinators	fluctuations
underscores	reproduction	diversity
study	species	abundance
monitoring	biodiversity	impacts
assess	ecosystem	habitat loss
understanding	stability	climate change
is	lifecycle	pesticide use
implementing	metamorphosis	factors
aimed	egg	conservation strategies
preserving	caterpillar	services
	pupa	
Nouns	butterfly	*Modifiers*
butterflies	adaptability	fascinating
subjects	resilience	ecological

pivotal	supporting	adult
environmental	characterized	invaluable
countless	final	

General Vocabulary

The vocabulary is technical and analytical, focusing on scientific aspects of butterflies and their ecological roles.

Unique Characteristics

This passage uses a formal and objective tone, providing a detailed analysis

Sentence Structure Characteristics

Complex Sentences: Often include multiple clauses to present detailed analysis (e.g., "Scientists study butterfly populations as indicators of environmental health...").

Formal Tone: Uses formal language suitable for analytical writing (e.g., "pivotal role," "sensitivity to environmental changes").

Evidence-Based: Provides evidence and examples to support analysis (e.g., "thereby supporting biodiversity and ecosystem stability").

Blog Paragraph

Passage

Butterflies are some of nature's most captivating creatures, known for their vibrant wings and delicate flight. Belonging to the order Lepidoptera, they undergo a remarkable four-stage life cycle: egg, larva (caterpillar), pupa (chrysalis), and adult. This process of metamorphosis allows them to adapt to different environments and roles throughout their lives. Butterflies are essential pollinators, helping plants reproduce by transferring pollen as they feed on nectar. Their presence also serves as a valuable indicator of ecosystem health. However, many butterfly populations are in decline due to habitat loss, pesticide use, and climate change, making conservation efforts increasingly important.

Average sentence length

Most sentences are medium length (around 18–25 words). Sentence 2 is slightly longer, listing stages, but overall sentences maintain clarity and flow.

Verbs
are
known
belonging
undergo
allows
adapt
are
helping
reproduce
transferring
feed
serves
are
decline
making

Nouns
butterflies
nature
creatures
wings
flight
order
life cycle
egg
larva
caterpillar
pupa
chrysalis
adult
process
metamorphosis
environments
roles
pollinators
plants
pollen
nectar
presence
indicator
ecosystem health
populations
habitat loss
pesticide use
climate change
conservation efforts

Modifiers
vibrant
delicate
remarkable
essential
valuable
increasingly important

General vocabulary

Vocabulary is formal but accessible, avoiding jargon without oversimplifying. Terms are precise and relevant to biology/ecology, making it informative and credible. Nouns are scientific and ecological, reflecting an educational tone. Terms like *Lepidoptera, metamorphosis,* and *ecosystem* give it authority. Moderate use of modifiers, mostly adjectives and descriptive phrases.

Unique Characteristics

The genre (informational blog) calls for clear, accessible modifiers that engage without overwhelming. The use of scientific classification (Order Lepidoptera) and terminology (pollinators, metamorphosis) signals informational writing aimed at a general audience interested in nature. The paragraph ends with a call action (importance of conservation), common in blogs addressing environmental topics. The verbs mostly describe states and processes (are, known, undergo, allows) and actions (helping, transferring, feed). This mix reflects a descriptive and explanatory genre focusing on informing rather than storytelling.

Sentence Structure Characteristics

Mostly declarative sentences with a simple subject-verb-object pattern or slight complexity due to modifiers or phrases.

Some sentences use colon for listing (life cycle stages).

Business Writing

Passage

Butterflies, as symbols of transformation and beauty, can be effectively integrated into branding strategies to convey themes of growth and change. Incorporating butterfly imagery in marketing materials such as logos, advertisements, and promotional campaigns can evoke positive emotions and resonate with audiences seeking renewal or innovation. Businesses can leverage the butterfly's symbolism to highlight product evolution, rebranding efforts, or organizational milestones. Additionally, using butterflies in corporate social responsibility initiatives, such as supporting pollinator conservation projects, can enhance a company's environmental stewardship image. Ultimately, integrating butterflies into business narratives can create memorable and impactful storytelling opportunities that connect with consumers on a deeper level.

Average Sentence Length

There are 6 sentences. Total word count is 106 words, so the average sentence length is 17.7 words per sentence.

Verbs
can be
integrated
convey
incorporating
evoke
resonate
seeking
leverage
highlight
supporting
enhance
integrating
create
connect

Nouns
butterflies
symbols
transformation
beauty
branding strategies
themes
growth
change
imagery
marketing materials
logos
advertisements
campaigns
emotions
audiences
renewal
innovation
businesses
symbolism
product evolution
rebranding efforts
organizational milestones
initiatives
projects
company
stewardship
image
narratives
storytelling opportunities
consumers
level

Modifiers
effectively
positive

corporate	memorable	deeper
environmental	impactful	

General Vocabulary

The vocabulary is professional and business-oriented, focusing on marketing and branding concepts.

Unique Characteristics

This passage uses a professional and strategic tone, providing practical advice for integrating butterflies into business branding. It emphasizes symbolism and consumer engagement.

Sentence Structure Characteristics

Directive and Suggestive: Offers suggestions and directives (e.g., "can be effectively integrated," "Businesses can leverage").

Purposeful Language: Uses language aimed at achieving specific business goals (e.g., "evoke positive emotions," "highlight product evolution").

Professional Tone: Maintains a professional and persuasive tone (e.g., "enhance a company's environmental stewardship image").

Copywriting

Passage

Discover the enchanting world of butterflies, where beauty meets grace in every delicate wingbeat. Dive into a kaleidoscope of colors and patterns that paint the air with elegance and wonder. Embrace the symbolism of transformation and renewal that butterflies embody, resonating with themes of growth and change. Experience the magic of nature's gentle messengers as they flutter through gardens, parks, and wild meadows. Let butterflies inspire your journey towards beauty, harmony, and the endless possibilities of the natural world.

Average Sentence Length

There are 5 sentences. Total word count is 84 words, so the average sentence length is approximately 16.8 words per sentence.

Verbs
discover
meets
dive
paint
embrace
embody
resonating
experience
flutter
let
inspire

Nouns
world
butterflies
beauty
grace
wingbeat
kaleidoscope
colors
patterns
air
elegance
wonder
symbolism
transformation
renewal
themes
growth
change
magic
messengers
gardens
parks
meadows
journey
harmony
possibilities
world

Modifiers
enchanting
delicate
elegant
gentle
wild
endless
natural

General Vocabulary

The vocabulary is evocative and persuasive, aiming to inspire and captivate the audience.

Unique Characteristics

This passage uses vivid imagery and emotional appeal to connect with the reader, typical of marketing and promotional writing. It emphasizes beauty, transformation, and inspiration.

Sentence Structure Characteristics

Invitational Language: Uses imperatives and emotionally evocative language (e.g., "Discover," "Embrace," "Experience").

Positive Imagery: Paints a vivid picture with descriptive and sensory language (e.g., "kaleidoscope of colors," "gentle messengers").

Rhetorical Devices: Employs rhetorical questions or statements to engage the reader (e.g., "Let butterflies inspire your journey...").

Creative Writing

Passage

In the quiet of dawn, a garden awakens with the gentle flutter of butterfly wings. Each delicate creature emerges from its chrysalis, unfolding vibrant patterns that rival the flowers they visit. Amongst the blossoms, a dance ensues, a choreography of colors that paints the air with fleeting beauty. Sunlight catches iridescent scales, casting a kaleidoscope of shimmering hues across the petals. As the day unfolds, these ephemeral messengers of summer weave tales of transformation and renewal, reminding all who witness their flight of the delicate balance and enduring magic of nature.

Average Sentence Length

There are 5 sentences. Total word count is 91 words, so the average sentence length is 18.2 words per sentence.

Verbs
awakens
emerges
unfolding
rival
visit
ensues
paints
catches
casting
unfolds
weave
reminding

Nouns
quiet
dawn
garden
flutter
wings
creature
chrysalis
patterns
flowers
blossoms
dance
choreography
colors
beauty
sunlight
scales
kaleidoscope
hues
petals
day
messengers
summer
tales
transformation
renewal
balance
magic
nature

Modifiers
quiet
gentle
delicate
vibrant
fleeting
iridescent
shimmering
ephemeral
delicate
enduring

General Vocabulary

The vocabulary is vivid and imaginative, focusing on visual and sensory imagery.

Unique Characteristics

This passage uses poetic and evocative language to create a rich, sensory experience for the reader. It emphasizes beauty and transformation, common themes in creative writing.

Sentence Structure Characteristics

Imagery-Rich Sentences: Uses vivid imagery to create a picturesque scene (e.g., "a garden awakens with the gentle flutter of butterfly wings").

Metaphorical Language: Employs metaphor and simile (e.g., "a choreography of colors," "messengers of summer").

Flowing Narrative: Sentences flow smoothly to create a rhythmic and lyrical quality (e.g., "a dance ensues, a choreography of colors that paints the air with fleeting beauty").

Descriptive Writing

Passage

In a sun-dappled meadow, butterflies dance gracefully on the gentle breeze. Their wings, adorned with vibrant patterns of orange, black, and iridescent blue, shimmer in the sunlight. With delicate movements, they flit from flower to flower, sipping nectar with slender proboscises. Each butterfly species displays unique wing patterns, from the majestic monarch with its bold stripes to the ethereal swallowtail adorned with delicate spots. As they flutter among blossoms, their presence adds a touch of enchantment to the tranquil scene, embodying the ephemeral beauty of nature's winged wonders.

Average Sentence Length

There are 5 sentences. Total word count is 87 words, so the average sentence length is about 17.4 words per sentence.

Verbs
dance
adorned
shimmer
flit
sipping
displays
flutter
adds
embodying

Nouns
meadow
butterflies
breeze
wings
patterns
orange
black
blue
sunlight
movements
flower
nectar
proboscises
species
wing
monarch
stripes
swallowtail
spots
blossoms
presence
touch
enchantment
scene
beauty
wonders

Modifiers
sun-dappled
gracefully
gentle
vibrant
iridescent
delicate
unique
majestic
bold
ethereal
delicate (repeated)
tranquil
ephemeral
winged

General Vocabulary

The vocabulary used is vivid and descriptive, focusing on visual and sensory imagery.

Unique Characteristics

This passage is rich with adjectives and adverbs, creating a vivid picture of butterflies in a meadow. The language is poetic, with a strong emphasis on the beauty and delicate nature of butterflies.

Sentence Structure Characteristics

Descriptive Imagery: Sentences often start with a scene or image (e.g., "In a sun-dappled meadow," "With delicate movements").

Modifiers: Rich use of adjectives and adverbs (e.g., "sun-dappled," "gracefully," "delicate").

Parallel Structure: Used to list attributes or actions (e.g., "Their wings, adorned with vibrant patterns of orange, black, and iridescent blue, shimmer in the sunlight").

Expository Writing

Passage

Butterflies belong to the order Lepidoptera and are known for their distinctive life cycle and ecological significance. They start their journey as eggs laid on specific host plants, where they hatch into larvae known as caterpillars. During this stage, caterpillars consume plant material voraciously to fuel their growth. After a period of feeding, they undergo metamorphosis inside a protective chrysalis, where they transform into adult butterflies. As adults, butterflies play a crucial role in pollination by transferring pollen from flower to flower as they feed on nectar. Their diverse habitats range from meadows and forests to urban gardens, showcasing their adaptability and importance in maintaining ecosystem health.

Average Sentence Length

There are 6 sentences. Total word count is 105 words, so the average sentence length is about 17.5 words per sentence.

Verbs
belong
are known
start
laid
hatch
consume
undergo
transform
play
transferring
feed
range
showcasing

Nouns
Butterflies
order
Lepidoptera
life cycle
significance
journey
eggs
plants
larvae
caterpillars
stage
material
growth
period
metamorphosis
chrysalis
adults
role
pollination
pollen
flower
nectar
habitats
meadows
forests
gardens
adaptability
importance
ecosystem
health

Modifiers
distinctive
specific
host
voraciously
protective
adult
crucial
diverse
urban
ecological

General Vocabulary

The vocabulary is informative and straightforward, focusing on the biological and ecological aspects of butterflies.

Unique Characteristics

This passage is factual and structured, with a clear progression through the butterfly's life cycle. The language is precise and technical, suitable for conveying scientific information.

Sentence Structure Characteristics

Informative Tone: Sentences present factual information clearly (e.g., "Butterflies belong to the order Lepidoptera").

Sequential Structure: Chronological order used to explain processes (e.g., "They start their journey as eggs...").

Complex Sentences: Often include subordinate clauses to provide additional details (e.g., "where they hatch into larvae known as caterpillars").

Journalistic Writing

Passage

Recent studies have shown a concerning decline in butterfly populations across various regions due to habitat loss and climate change. Scientists from leading research institutions are conducting extensive field studies to understand the factors contributing to this decline. Experts emphasize the critical role of butterflies as indicators of environmental health, highlighting their importance in ecosystems worldwide. Conservation efforts are intensifying, with organizations collaborating to protect butterfly habitats and promote sustainable practices. As public awareness grows, initiatives are being launched to engage communities in butterfly monitoring and habitat restoration projects to safeguard these iconic insects for future generations.

Average Sentence Length

There are 5 sentences. Total word count is 90 words, so the average sentence length is 18 words per sentence.

Verbs
have shown
conducting
understand
contributing
emphasize
highlighting
are intensifying
collaborating
promote
grows
are being launched
engage
safeguard

Nouns
studies
decline
populations
regions
habitat loss
climate change
scientists
institutions
field studies
factors
decline
experts
role
indicators
health
importance
ecosystems
efforts
organizations
habitats
practices
awareness
initiatives
communities
monitoring
restoration projects
insects
generations

Modifiers
recent
concerning
various
extensive
critical
environmental
worldwide
sustainable
iconic
future

General Vocabulary

The vocabulary is formal and informative, focusing on current events and scientific findings.

Unique Characteristics

This passage uses an objective and informative tone, typical of journalistic writing. It reports on current research and conservation efforts, emphasizing the urgency of the issue.

Sentence Structure Characteristics

Objective Reporting: Presents factual information without personal bias (e.g., "Recent studies have shown," "Scientists are conducting extensive field studies").

Sequential Information: Describes events or actions in a chronological or logical order (e.g., "Conservation efforts are intensifying").

Expert Opinion: Includes statements from experts to support claims (e.g., "Experts emphasize the critical role of butterflies").

Narrative Writing

Passage

As I wandered through the sunlit garden, I noticed a flutter of movement out of the corner of my eye. Curious, I followed the delicate creature as it danced among the blooming flowers. Its wings, adorned with hues of orange and black, shimmered in the golden afternoon light. Mesmerized by its graceful flight, I watched as it alighted on a nearby blossom, delicately sipping nectar with its slender proboscis. For a fleeting moment, the world seemed to slow down, encapsulated by the beauty and tranquility of this enchanting encounter with nature's airborne marvels.

Average Sentence Length

There are 5 sentences. Total word count is 87 words, so the average sentence length is about 17.4 words per sentence.

Verbs		*Modifiers*
wandered	creature	sunlit
noticed	flowers	flutter
followed	wings	corner
danced	hues	delicate
adorned	orange	blooming
shimmered	black	adorned
watched	light	orange
alighted	flight	black
sipping	blossom	golden
seemed	nectar	graceful
encapsulated	proboscis	nearby
	moment	delicately
	world	slender
Nouns	beauty	fleeting
garden	tranquility	slow
flutter	encounter	enchanting
movement	nature	airborne
corner	marvels	
eye		

General Vocabulary

The vocabulary is descriptive and personal, drawing the reader into a specific moment and experience.

Unique Characteristics

This passage uses a first-person perspective and emotive language, creating a personal and immersive experience. The descriptive elements evoke a sense of wonder and tranquility.

Sentence Structure Characteristics

First-Person Perspective: Use of "I" to create a personal narrative (e.g., "As I wandered through the sunlit garden").

Descriptive Detail: Rich, sensory descriptions (e.g., "shimmered in the golden afternoon light").

Temporal Structure: Describes actions in sequence to build a narrative (e.g., "Curious, I followed the delicate creature...").

Oral Presentation Script

Passage

Hello everyone! Today, I want to share some fascinating facts about butterflies. These beautiful insects go through an incredible transformation called metamorphosis, starting as eggs, then becoming caterpillars, forming a chrysalis, and finally emerging as colorful butterflies. They play a crucial role in nature by pollinating flowers, which helps plants reproduce and supports biodiversity. Butterflies are also sensitive to changes in the environment, making them important indicators of ecosystem health. Unfortunately, many species face threats like habitat loss and climate change. Protecting butterflies means protecting the balance of our natural world. Thank you!

Sentence length

Sentences are mostly short to medium, around 10–20 words, optimized for clear oral delivery.

Verbs		*Modifiers*
want	facts	fascinating
share	butterflies	beautiful
go	insects	incredible
called	transformation	crucial
starting	metamorphosis	colorful
becoming	eggs	important
forming	caterpillars	natural
emerging	chrysalis	
play	butterflies	
pollinating	role	
helps	nature	
supports	flowers	
are	plants	
making	biodiversity	
face	species	
protecting	threats	
means	habitat loss	
	climate change	
Nouns	balance	
everyone	world	

General vocabulary

Vocabulary is conversational and clear, designed for an oral format. Uses everyday words and phrases like "fascinating facts" and "protecting the balance," which are motivational and accessible. Vocabulary is simple and familiar, reflecting the need to connect with a general audience in a spoken context. Verbs are mostly active and dynamic (go, become, form, emerge, play), suitable for spoken explanation and keeping attention. Light to moderate use of adjectives, with emotive and positive tone: Modifiers serve to engage listeners and maintain interest.

Unique Characteristics

Presence of direct address ("Hello everyone!") and closing ("Thank you!") are typical oral presentation markers. Emphasis on engagement, clarity, and motivation, matching a spoken informational style.

Sentence structure Characteristics

Uses simple and compound sentences for clarity and rhythm in speech. Includes lists and sequences with "starting as eggs, then becoming…" for easy following.

Personal Writing

Passage
Butterflies have always held a special place in my heart since childhood, when I would chase them through sunlit fields, marveling at their ethereal beauty. Their graceful dance among flowers never fails to lift my spirits and remind me of life's fleeting yet profound moments. I find solace in watching them flit from bloom to bloom, each one a tiny masterpiece of nature's design. As I've grown older, I've come to appreciate their symbolic significance of transformation and resilience, mirroring my own journey of growth and adaptation. For me, butterflies symbolize hope, reminding me to embrace change and find beauty in every stage of life's metamorphosis.

Average Sentence Length
There are 5 sentences. Total word count is 106 words, so the average sentence length is approximately 21.2 words per sentence.

Verbs	place	hope
have held	heart	change
would chase	childhood	beauty
marveling	fields	stage
fails	beauty	life
lift	dance	metamorphosis
remind	flowers	
find	spirits	*Modifiers*
flit	moments	special
grown	solace	my
come	bloom	sunlit
appreciate	masterpiece	ethereal
mirroring	nature	graceful
symbolize	design	fleeting
reminding	significance	profound
embrace	transformation	tiny
find	resilience	symbolic
	journey	own
Nouns	growth	ever
butterflies	adaptation	

General Vocabulary

The vocabulary is reflective and personal, aimed at expressing deep emotions and experiences. Words like "ethereal," "graceful," "solace," and "metamorphosis" add a poetic and introspective quality to the writing.

Unique Characteristics

Emotional and Reflective Tone: The writing is deeply personal and introspective, expressing a strong emotional connection to butterflies.

Descriptive Language: Vivid descriptions such as "sunlit fields," "ethereal beauty," "graceful dance," and "tiny masterpiece" create a picturesque and emotive imagery.

Symbolism and Metaphor: Butterflies are used symbolically to represent hope, transformation, resilience, and life's stages. This metaphorical use enriches the passage and adds layers of meaning.

First-Person Perspective: The use of first-person perspective ("my heart," "I would chase," "I find solace") makes the writing intimate and relatable.

Flow and Cohesion: The sentences are well-connected, creating a smooth narrative flow that enhances the readability and emotional impact.

Sentence Structure Characteristics

Reflective and Introspective: Focuses on personal experiences and emotions (e.g., "Butterflies have always held a special place in my heart").

Sensory Detail: Includes vivid descriptions to evoke emotions (e.g., "chase them through sunlit fields," "watching them flit from bloom to bloom").

Philosophical Theme: Explores deeper meanings and life lessons (e.g., "For me, butterflies symbolize hope").

Persuasive Writing

Passage

Butterflies are not just delicate and beautiful creatures; they are essential pollinators that play a crucial role in maintaining biodiversity and food security. Their ability to transfer pollen from one plant to another helps fertilize flowers, enabling them to produce fruits and seeds. Without butterflies, many plant species would struggle to reproduce, affecting entire ecosystems. By conserving butterfly habitats and promoting pollinator-friendly practices, we can ensure their continued presence and contribute to sustainable agriculture. Protecting butterflies also benefits other wildlife that depend on these insects for food and contributes to the overall health of our planet. Therefore, it is imperative that we recognize and safeguard the importance of butterflies in our environment.

Average Sentence Length

There are 6 sentences. Total word count is 113 words, so the average sentence length is about 18.8 words per sentence.

Verbs	safeguard	agriculture
are		wildlife
play	*Nouns*	insects
transfer	butterflies	health
helps	creatures	planet
enabling	pollinators	importance
produce	role	environment
struggle	biodiversity	
reproduce	food security	*Modifiers*
affecting	ability	delicate
conserving	pollen	beautiful
promoting	plant	essential
ensure	flowers	crucial
contribute	fruits	one
protecting	seeds	entire
benefits	species	pollinator-friendly
depend	ecosystems	continued
contributes	habitats	sustainable
recognize	practices	overall

General Vocabulary

The vocabulary is persuasive and emphasizes the ecological importance and benefits of butterflies.

Unique Characteristics

This passage uses a persuasive tone, highlighting the importance of butterflies to ecosystems and human agriculture. It employs logical arguments and appeals to the reader's sense of responsibility.

Sentence Structure Characteristics

Argumentative Structure: Presents a claim and supports it with reasons and evidence (e.g., "Butterflies are not just delicate and beautiful creatures; they are essential pollinators...").

Appeals to Logic and Emotion: Combines factual information with emotional appeal (e.g., "Protecting butterflies also benefits other wildlife...").

Imperative Sentences: Directs readers to take action (e.g., "By conserving butterfly habitats...").

Review Writing

Passage

In Pursuit of Butterflies by Matthew Oates is a captivating blend of natural history and memoir, chronicling the author's lifelong passion for these enchanting insects. Oates brings a poetic touch to his detailed observations, immersing readers in the vibrant world of butterflies with vivid descriptions and personal anecdotes. His deep knowledge and enthusiasm shine through, making the science accessible and engaging for both experts and novices. The book also reflects on broader environmental issues, highlighting the importance of conservation. Overall, it's a delightful and insightful read that celebrates the beauty and complexity of butterflies.

Average Sentence Length

There are 6 sentences. Total word count is 90 words, so the average sentence length is 15 words per sentence.

Verbs
is
chronicling
brings
immersing
shine
making
reflects
highlighting
celebrates

Nouns
blend
history
memoir
passion
insects
touch
observations
readers
world
descriptions
anecdotes
knowledge
enthusiasm
science
experts
novices
book
issues
importance
conservation
read
beauty
complexity
butterflies

Modifiers
captivating
natural
lifelong
enchanting
poetic
detailed
vibrant
vivid
personal
deep
accessible
engaging
broader
environmental
delightful
insightful

General Vocabulary

The vocabulary is descriptive and evaluative, focusing on personal engagement and critique.

Unique Characteristics

This passage combines personal evaluation with factual information, providing both an overview of the book's content and an assessment of its impact. It uses emotive and engaging language to convey the reviewer's perspective.

Sentence Structure Characteristics

Evaluative and Descriptive: Combines evaluation with descriptive detail (e.g., "captivating blend of natural history and memoir").

Personal Perspective: Includes personal opinions and recommendations (e.g., "Overall, it's a delightful and insightful read").

Positive Adjectives: Uses positive adjectives to convey approval (e.g., "captivating," "poetic," "vivid").

Script Writing

Passage

[Scene: A sunny garden with colorful flowers swaying gently in the breeze. Two friends, Emma and David, are sitting on a bench, observing butterflies fluttering around.]

Emma: (pointing excitedly) Look at that butterfly! Its wings are so vibrant.

David: (nodding) Yeah, butterflies are amazing. Did you know they start as tiny eggs and go through a complete transformation?

Emma: (smiling) I read they're important pollinators too, helping plants grow by carrying pollen from one flower to another.

David: (leaning closer) It's fascinating how they navigate with such delicate wings. Imagine having to migrate thousands of miles like monarch butterflies do.

Emma: (reflecting) They're like nature's living art, each species with its own unique colors and patterns. It's incredible how something so small can have such a big impact on the environment.

David: (grinning) Absolutely. I think we should plant more butterfly-friendly flowers in our garden to attract them here.

Average Sentence Length

There are 9 sentences. Total word count is 103 words, so the average sentence length is approximately 11.4 words per sentence.

Verbs	smiling	migrate
pointing	read	reflecting
are	are	are
Look	helping	having
is	grow	do
nodding	carrying	grinning
know	leaning	think
start	navigate	should
go	imagine	plant

attract	pollinators	sunny
	plants	colorful
Nouns	pollen	gently
scene	flower	excitedly
garden	wings	vibrant
flowers	miles	tiny
breeze	monarch butterflies	complete
friends	art	important
Emma	species	delicate
David	colors	thousands
bench	patterns	unique
butterflies	environment	small
wings	flowers	big
eggs		butterfly-friendly
transformation	*Modifiers*	

General Vocabulary

The vocabulary is conversational and straightforward, aiming to simulate a natural dialogue.

Unique Characteristics

This passage uses dialogue to convey information in a relatable and engaging way. It combines factual content with personal reflections, making it accessible and easy to follow.

Sentence Structure Characteristics

Dialogue Format: Presented as a conversation between characters (Emma and David).

Casual Tone: Uses informal language suitable for spoken communication (e.g., "Did you know," "It's fascinating").

Character Interaction: Includes gestures and actions to depict a scene (e.g., "pointing excitedly," "leaning closer").

Summary

Passage
Butterflies are colorful insects known for their four-stage life cycle: egg, caterpillar, chrysalis, and adult. This metamorphosis allows them to adapt and thrive in various environments. As important pollinators, butterflies help plants reproduce by transferring pollen while feeding on nectar. Their presence also serves as an indicator of environmental health, as they are sensitive to habitat changes and climate shifts. Unfortunately, many butterfly species are declining due to habitat loss, pesticide use, and global warming. Protecting butterflies is essential not only for their survival but also for maintaining biodiversity and the health of ecosystems worldwide.

Sentence length
Sentences are mostly medium length, between 15–22 words, typical for summaries—concise but complete.

Verbs	insects	habitat loss
are	life cycle	pesticide use
known	egg	global warming
allows	caterpillar	survival
adapt	chrysalis	biodiversity
thrive	adult	health
help	metamorphosis	ecosystems
reproduce	environments	
transferring	pollinators	*Modifiers*
feeding	plants	colorful
serves	pollen	four-stage
are	nectar	important
declining	presence	environmental
Protecting	indicator	butterfly
is	environmental health	many
	habitat changes	essential
Nouns	climate shifts	biodiversity
butterflies	species	global

General Vocabulary

Vocabulary is formal, clear, and neutral, without emotive or persuasive language, fitting a summary genre. Vocabulary is scientific and precise, appropriate for a brief factual overview. Verbs mostly describe states and processes, emphasizing facts and cause-effect relationships—typical for a summary. Moderate use of clear, factual modifiers. Modifiers are functional, adding precision without ornamentation.

Unique Characteristics

Lack of personal address or emotional appeal identifies this as a neutral, objective summary.

Focus on key facts and implications without extra commentary or narrative.

Sentence Structure Characteristics

Mostly simple and compound sentences, straightforward and to the point. Information is compressed for efficient communication.

Technical Writing

Passage

In the realm of entomology, butterflies (order Lepidoptera) are revered for their intricate life cycle and diverse ecological roles. Starting as eggs laid on specific host plants, these insects undergo metamorphosis through four distinct stages: egg, larva (caterpillar), pupa (chrysalis), and adult. During the larval stage, caterpillars feed voraciously on plant foliage, storing energy for their transformation. The pupal stage marks a period of dramatic change, where the caterpillar undergoes complete restructuring inside the chrysalis before emerging as a fully formed adult butterfly. As adults, butterflies play crucial roles in pollination and serve as indicators of environmental health due to their sensitivity to habitat changes. Studying butterflies aids in understanding biodiversity, ecosystem dynamics, and the impacts of climate change on insect populations.

Average Sentence Length

There are 6 sentences. Total word count is 104 words, so the average sentence length is approximately 17.3 words per sentence.

Verbs	order	transformation
are revered	Lepidoptera	period
starting	life cycle	change
laid	roles	restructuring
undergo	eggs	adult butterfly
feed	host plants	roles
storing	insects	pollination
marks	metamorphosis	indicators
undergoes	stages	health
emerging	egg	sensitivity
play	larva	habitat changes
serve	caterpillar	biodiversity
aids	pupa	ecosystem dynamics
	chrysalis	impacts
Nouns	adult	climate change
realm	stage	populations
entomology	plant foliage	
butterflies	energy	*Modifiers*

intricate	larval	fully formed
diverse	voraciously	crucial
specific	dramatic	environmental
distinct	complete	

General Vocabulary

The vocabulary is specialized and scientific, appropriate for an academic or technical audience.

Unique Characteristics

This passage is precise and informative, using technical terms and a structured explanation to describe the life cycle and ecological significance of butterflies.

Sentence Structure Characteristics

Technical Detail: Provides precise and detailed information (e.g., "Starting as eggs laid on specific host plants," "metamorphosis through four distinct stages").

Definition and Classification: Uses specific terminology (e.g., "order Lepidoptera," "larva (caterpillar), pupa (chrysalis), and adult").

Cause and Effect: Explains processes or phenomena with clear cause-effect relationships (e.g., "Due to their sensitivity to habitat changes").

Travel Writing

Passage

In the lush rainforests of Central America, butterflies thrive amidst a kaleidoscope of tropical flora. Wander through the Cloud Forest Reserve, where vibrant species like the morpho butterfly adorn the forest canopy with flashes of electric blue. Explore the Amazon rainforest in Brazil, where diverse habitats host a dazzling array of butterfly species, from the striking heliconians to the delicate glasswings. Journey to the butterfly sanctuaries of Mexico's Michoacán region, where millions of monarch butterflies gather annually in a breathtaking spectacle of migration and conservation. Whether in the misty mountains of Asia or the sunny savannas of Africa, butterflies enchant travelers with their beauty and ecological significance, making them a must-see on any nature lover's itinerary.

Average Sentence Length

There are 5 sentences. Total word count is 103 words, so the average sentence length is approximately 20.6 words per sentence.

Verbs	morpho butterfly	Asia
thrive	canopy	savannas
wander	flashes	Africa
adorn	electric blue	travelers
explore	Amazon rainforest	beauty
host	Brazil	ecological significance
journey	habitats	nature lover's itinerary
gather	array	
making	species	*Modifiers*
enchant	heliconians	lush
	glasswings	tropical
Nouns	sanctuaries	vibrant
rainforests	Mexico's Michoacán region	dazzling
Central America		striking
butterflies	monarch butterflies	delicate
kaleidoscope	spectacle	breathtaking
flora	migration	misty
Cloud Forest Reserve	conservation	sunny
species	mountains	must-see

General Vocabulary

The vocabulary is descriptive and evocative, aimed at painting vivid images and evoking a sense of adventure.

Unique Characteristics

This passage uses rich, descriptive language to captivate the reader and evoke a sense of wonder and excitement about travel. It highlights specific destinations and species, emphasizing both beauty and ecological importance.

Sentence Structure Characteristics

Descriptive Imagery: Paints vivid pictures of locations and scenes (e.g., "lush rainforests," "dazzling array of butterfly species").

Location-Based Details: Mentions specific places and attractions (e.g., "Cloud Forest Reserve," "butterfly sanctuaries of Mexico's Michoacán region").

Engaging Narrative: Invites readers to explore and experience different environments (e.g., "Whether in the misty mountains...").

Summary Table:

Aspect	Academic Writing	Analytical Writing	Blog	Business Writing	Copywriting	Creative Writing	Descriptive Writing	Expository Writing	Journalistic Writing
Other markers	Objective tone, scientific framing	Explanatory depth; connects evidence to evaluation	Scientific references, call to action	Brand image, consumer appeal	Invitational, evocative language	Symbolism, transformation, emotion	Rich imagery, sensory detail	Sequential process; neutral voice	Quotes from experts, studies, initiatives
Sentence length	Medium (15–20 words)	Long (18–25 words); dense	Medium (18–25 words)	Medium (16–20 words)	Medium (16–17 words)	Medium (15–20 words)	Medium (17–18 words)	Medium (16–20 words); sequential	Medium (16–20 words)
Use of modifiers	Light to moderate; technical	Moderate; technical and analytical	Moderate; descriptive, scientific	Light; strategic, professional	Evocative, persuasive	Rich; poetic, sensory	Heavy; vivid, sensory, adjective-rich	Moderate; clear, sequential	Moderate; precise, factual
Verbs	States/ process; formal	States/ process + analytic actions	Mix of states/ process + some actions	Suggestive, strategic	Evocative, inviting	Active and descriptive	Active, sensory, descriptive	Process-based, explanatory	States/ process; evidence-based
Nouns	Scientific, domain-specific	Scientific, abstract, evaluative	Scientific/ecological terms	Marketing and brand-related	Vivid, emotive	Nature-based and symbolic	Visual and sensory imagery	Scientific, ecological, and functional	Scientific, institutional, environmental
Vocabulary	Technical and precise	Technical, analytical, evidence-driven	Formal but accessible	Professional, strategic	Evocative, inspirational	Poetic, imaginative	Vivid, descriptive, sensory	Informative, structured, biological	Formal, precise, technical
Sentence structure	Complex; definition-elaboration	Complex; multi-clause, analytical reasoning	Declarative, lists, complex	Directive and purpose-driven	Invitational, rhetorical	Flowing, lyrical	Parallel structure, rich imagery	Chronological; logical progression	Objective, factual, multi-source reporting

Aspect	Narrative Writing	Oral Presentation	Personal Writing	Persuasive Writing	Review Writing	Script Writing	Summary	Technical Writing	Travel Writing
Other markers	First-person perspective, emotion	Direct address, engagement markers	First-person, introspective	Call to action, evaluative language	Reviewer stance, subjective analysis	Dialogue, gestures, casual tone	Neutral tone, factual summary	Technical terms, precise details	Location details, vivid imagery
Sentence length	Medium (15-20 words)	Short to medium (10-20 words)	Medium (20-22 words)	Medium to long (18-25 words)	Medium (14-18 words)	Short (10-12 words)	Medium (15-22 words)	Medium (17-18 words)	Medium (19-21 words)
Use of modifiers	Heavy; vivid, sensory	Light to moderate; engaging, positive	Reflective, emotive	Moderate, emphatic, evaluative	Moderate; descriptive, evaluative	Light, conversational	Moderate; clear, factual	Technical, precise, structured	Rich, descriptive
Verbs	Active and emotional	Mostly active and dynamic	Reflective, personal	Active and persuasive	Mix of states/process and evaluation	Conversational, explanatory	Mostly states/process	Precise, process-focused	Descriptive, engaging
Nouns	Personal and nature-based imagery	Simple, familiar terms	Personal, symbolic	Conceptual and ecological	Literary and critical	Everyday, concrete	Scientific, precise	Scientific, technical	Geographical, species-focused
Vocabulary	Descriptive, personal, emotive	Conversational, clear	Poetic, reflective	Persuasive, cause-oriented	Evaluative, expressive	Clear, natural	Formal, neutral	Formal, precise, technical	Descriptive, immersive
Sentence structure	First-person; sensory, chronological	Simple/compound, conversational	Reflective, connected	Argumentative; cause-effect; imperative	Descriptive; includes assessment	Dialogue-driven	Simple/compound, factual	Structured, detailed	Descriptive, narrative

4. Which genres are persuasive? Use the above sample paragraphs, think further about the genre, then put a check mark next to each persuasive genre. Note that some genres *can* be persuasive while others are generally persuasive. Promoting an argument is a form of persuasion.

- ✓ Academic writing
- ✓ Analytical writing
- ✓ Blog (probably)
- ✓ Business writing
- ✓ Copywriting
- Creative writing
- ✓ Descriptive writing (maybe)
- ✓ Expository writing
- ✓ Journalistic writing
- ✓ Narrative writing (maybe)
- ✓ Oral presentation
- ✓ Personal writing (maybe)
- ✓ Persuasive writing
- ✓ Review writing
- ✓ Script writing (maybe)
- Summary
- ✓ Technical writing (probably)
- ✓ Travel writing

Sometimes the persuasion is simply *I'm right about this; believe me.*

29. logos, ethos, and pathos

Which genres of writing correspond with the seven possible combinations of *logos*, *ethos*, and *pathos*?

A. strong logos, weak ethos, weak pathos
Technical Writing

Strong Logos: Technical writing emphasizes logical reasoning, facts, data, and detailed information. It aims to explain complex ideas clearly and concisely, relying heavily on evidence and systematic presentation of information.

Weak Ethos: While the credibility of the information is important, technical writing often assumes that the reader trusts the accuracy of the data and the methodology used to obtain it. It focuses less on the author's character or reputation.

Weak Pathos: Emotional appeal is generally minimal in technical writing. The primary goal is to inform or instruct, not to persuade or evoke an emotional response.

Examples include instruction manuals, scientific reports, and technical documentation.

B. weak logos, strong ethos, weak pathos

Memoir writing

Weak Logos: Memoir writing often does not rely heavily on logical reasoning or structured arguments. Instead, it focuses on personal experiences and reflections, which may not follow a strict logical structure or be supported by extensive evidence.

Strong Ethos: The credibility and character of the author are central to memoir writing. The author's personal experiences, insights, and authenticity are what engage the reader and give the narrative its power.

Weak Pathos: While memoirs can evoke emotions, the primary focus is not on manipulating the reader's emotions but rather on sharing genuine experiences and personal growth.

Memoirs are personal accounts that provide insight into the author's life and perspective, relying on the author's credibility and unique voice to engage readers.

C. weak logos, weak ethos, strong pathos

Poetry

Weak Logos: Poetry often does not rely on logical reasoning or structured arguments. Instead, it prioritizes artistic expression, imagery, and emotional impact over factual accuracy or logical consistency.

Weak Ethos: The credibility of the poet is usually not the focus. Readers are more interested in the emotional and aesthetic experience than the qualifications or character of the poet.

Strong Pathos: Poetry is highly effective in evoking emotions. Through the use of figurative language, metaphor, rhythm, and other literary devices, poetry aims to stir feelings and create a profound emotional experience for the reader.

Poetry uses its unique form and style to connect with readers on a deeply emotional level, often prioritizing the conveyance of feelings and experiences over factual or logical presentation.

D. strong logos, strong ethos, weak pathos

Genres of writing that typically use strong logos, strong ethos, and weak pathos include technical writing, scientific writing, and academic writing.

1. Academic Writing:

Strong Logos: Academic writing involves well-reasoned arguments, supported by evidence and logical analysis. It aims to contribute to scholarly discourse and advance knowledge.

Strong Ethos: The author's expertise, thorough research, and adherence to academic standards establish credibility and authority.

Weak Pathos: Academic writing prioritizes objectivity and rationality over emotional appeal, focusing on presenting information and arguments logically and coherently.

2. Scientific Writing:

Strong Logos: Scientific writing is grounded in empirical evidence, logical analysis, and methodological rigor. It presents research findings, theories, and data in a structured and logical manner.

Strong Ethos: The reputation and credentials of the author(s) are important, as they establish trust and authority in the scientific community.

Weak Pathos: Scientific writing aims to be objective and neutral, avoiding emotional language to maintain impartiality and credibility.

3. Technical Writing:

Strong Logos: Technical writing relies heavily on logical structure, clear explanations, and factual information. It aims to inform or instruct the reader about specific procedures, technologies, or processes.

Strong Ethos: The credibility of the author is crucial in technical writing. Authors are often experts in their field, and their qualifications lend authority to the document.

Weak Pathos: Emotional appeal is minimal or absent in technical writing. The focus is on clarity, precision, and utility rather than evoking emotions.

These genres prioritize logical reasoning and credibility while minimizing emotional appeal to maintain objectivity and professionalism.

E. weak logos, strong ethos, strong pathos

Genres of writing that typically use weak logos (logic), strong ethos (credibility), and strong pathos (emotion) include:

1. Advertisement and Marketing Copy:

Weak Logos: Advertising and marketing often use persuasion techniques, catchy slogans, and emotional appeals to sell products or promote ideas, rather than rigorous logical arguments.

Strong Ethos: The credibility in marketing comes from the brand's reputation, endorsements, and persuasive tactics used to build trust and authority.

Strong Pathos: Advertisements and marketing campaigns frequently leverage emotional triggers, such as happiness, fear, nostalgia, or desire, to influence consumer behavior.

2. Creative Writing (Fiction, Poetry):

Weak Logos: Creative writing may prioritize imaginative storytelling, literary devices, and narrative structure over factual accuracy or logical argumentation.

Strong Ethos: The credibility in creative writing stems from the author's literary skill, creativity, and ability to engage the reader through artistic expression.

Strong Pathos: Fiction and poetry often aim to elicit deep emotional responses from readers through vivid descriptions, character development, and thematic exploration.

3. Personal Writing (Memoirs, Personal Essays):

Weak Logos: Personal writing often prioritizes personal experiences, anecdotes, and subjective perspectives over logical argumentation or factual evidence.

Strong Ethos: The credibility in personal writing comes from the authenticity and sincerity of the author's voice and personal insights.

Strong Pathos: These genres aim to evoke strong emotions in the reader by sharing personal stories, reflections, and experiences that resonate emotionally.

4. Political Speeches and Campaigns:

Weak Logos: Political rhetoric often emphasizes persuasive language, ideological appeals, and emotional narratives rather than purely factual or logical arguments.

Strong Ethos: Political figures build credibility through their leadership qualities, experience, public persona, and alignment with the values of their supporters.

Strong Pathos: Political speeches and campaigns frequently use emotional appeals to rally supporters, evoke empathy, and mobilize voters based on shared beliefs or concerns.

5. Speeches (Motivational, Inspirational):

Weak Logos: Speeches, especially motivational or inspirational ones, may prioritize emotional storytelling, motivational anecdotes, and rhetorical devices over logical reasoning.

Strong Ethos: The credibility of the speaker is crucial in speeches, established through personal charisma, expertise, or authority on the topic.

Strong Pathos: These speeches aim to inspire or persuade audiences by tapping into their emotions, aspirations, or shared values.

These genres use strong ethos to establish credibility and strong pathos to evoke emotions effectively, while the logical appeal (logos) may take a back seat to storytelling, persuasion, or artistic expression.

F. strong logos, weak ethos, strong pathos

Genres of writing that typically use strong logos (logic), weak ethos (credibility), and strong pathos (emotion) include:

1. Advocacy and Activism Writing:

Strong Logos: Advocacy and activism writing uses logical reasoning, statistics, and evidence to support calls for action or change on social, political, or environmental issues.

Weak Ethos: The credibility in advocacy writing often comes from the cause or issue being championed rather than the individual author's credentials or authority.

Strong Pathos: These genres aim to mobilize readers emotionally, often using stories of hardship, injustice, or human suffering to elicit empathy and inspire action.

2. Campaign Speeches and Propaganda:

Strong Logos: Campaign speeches and propaganda often present logical arguments to persuade audiences of a candidate's platform, policies, or ideological stance.

Weak Ethos: While candidates or propagandists may have some credibility based on their positions or affiliations, the emphasis is more on crafting persuasive arguments rather than establishing personal credibility.

Strong Pathos: These genres use emotional appeals to rally supporters, create a sense of urgency, and provoke emotional responses that motivate action or allegiance.

3. Legal Writing (Arguments and Persuasion):

Strong Logos: Legal writing relies heavily on logical reasoning, case law, statutes, and legal precedents to construct persuasive arguments in court briefs, legal opinions, or arguments.

Weak Ethos: The credibility in legal writing is established through adherence to legal principles and rigorous argumentation rather than personal authority or character.

Strong Pathos: In certain legal contexts, emotional appeals may be used strategically to sway judges or juries, especially in cases involving human rights, justice, or morality.

    4. Opinion Columns and Editorial Writing:

Strong Logos: Opinion columns and editorials often rely on logical arguments, reasoning, and evidence to support a particular viewpoint or argument.

Weak Ethos: While some writers may have expertise in the subject matter, the emphasis is more on the strength of the argument presented rather than the author's personal credibility or authority.

Strong Pathos: These genres aim to evoke strong emotional responses from readers, often through passionate language, vivid descriptions, and appeals to values or beliefs.

    5. Proposals and Grant Applications:

Strong Logos: Proposals and grant applications use logical reasoning, data, and evidence to justify funding requests, project plans, or business initiatives.

Weak Ethos: The credibility in these documents is derived from the feasibility and merit of the proposal rather than the personal authority of the applicant or author.

Strong Pathos: These genres may include emotional appeals to demonstrate the potential impact of the proposed project or initiative, especially when addressing societal or humanitarian issues.

These genres prioritize strong logical arguments (logos) and effective emotional appeals (pathos) to persuade audiences, while the credibility of the author or speaker (ethos) may be less central to the persuasive strategy.

G. strong logos, strong ethos, strong pathos

Genres of writing that utilize strong logos (logic), strong ethos (credibility), and strong pathos (emotion) include:

    1. Documentaries and Films (Social Issues, Environmental Causes):

Strong Logos: Documentaries and films employ factual information, expert interviews, and visual evidence to provide a comprehensive exploration of complex issues.

Strong Ethos: Filmmakers and documentarians establish credibility through research, interviews with experts, and a commitment to journalistic integrity, enhancing the credibility of their narrative.

Strong Pathos: These mediums use storytelling, imagery, and personal narratives to evoke strong emotional responses, raise awareness, and inspire viewers to take action or reconsider their perspectives.

2. . Literary Fiction (Novels, Short Stories):

Strong Logos: Literary fiction uses narrative structure, character development, and thematic exploration to explore universal truths, social issues, or philosophical questions.

Strong Ethos: Authors establish credibility through their narrative skill, depth of character portrayal, and ability to illuminate human nature, gaining readers' trust in their storytelling.

Strong Pathos: These genres evoke empathy, compassion, and a range of emotions through compelling characters, evocative prose, and poignant storytelling that resonates on a deep emotional level.

3. Literary Nonfiction (Memoirs, Personal Essays):

Strong Logos: Literary nonfiction uses narrative techniques, anecdotes, and thematic exploration to convey truths or insights about life, society, or personal experience.

Strong Ethos: Authors build credibility through authenticity, introspection, and personal reflection, inviting readers to trust their perspective and insights.

Strong Pathos: These genres evoke powerful emotional responses by delving into universal human experiences, dilemmas, or struggles, resonating deeply with readers' emotions and empathy.

4. Persuasive Essays:

Strong Logos: Persuasive essays present well-reasoned arguments supported by evidence, facts, and logical reasoning to convince the reader of a particular viewpoint or stance.

Strong Ethos: Authors establish credibility through expertise on the subject matter, authoritative sources, or personal experience, enhancing the persuasiveness of their arguments.

Strong Pathos: These essays employ emotional appeals to engage readers' emotions, evoke empathy, or inspire action, reinforcing the logical arguments with emotional resonance.

5. Speeches (Political, Social Movements):

Strong Logos: Speeches use logical arguments, statistics, and examples to articulate a coherent message or agenda, often aiming to persuade or mobilize an audience.

Strong Ethos: Speakers establish credibility through their position, expertise, or leadership in the subject matter, enhancing the audience's trust in their message.

Strong Pathos: Effective speeches harness emotional appeals to connect with listeners on a personal level, stir feelings of solidarity or urgency, and galvanize support for a cause or idea.

These genres integrate strong logical arguments, credible authorship, and powerful emotional appeals to create persuasive, impactful, and emotionally resonant pieces of writing.

H. weak logos, weak ethos, weak pathos

Genres of writing that often rely on weak logos (logic), weak ethos (credibility), and weak pathos (emotion) tend to fall outside the realm of persuasive or analytical writing. These genres may focus more on entertainment, casual communication, or simplicity than on building strong arguments.

1. Elementary-Level Writing (Early Learning)

Weak Logos: May rely on repetition rather than reasoning.

Weak Ethos: Author's identity not a factor.

Weak Pathos: Simple emotions, if any.

Example: "The cat is big. The dog is fast." — designed for language development, not persuasion.

2. Instruction Manuals (Basic or Poorly Written)

Weak Logos: May provide steps without explaining reasoning or concepts.

Weak Ethos: Author or company credentials are rarely emphasized.

Weak Pathos: Typically emotionless and purely functional.

Example: "Step 3: Insert plug." — practical but uninspired and unsupported.

3. Social Media Captions and Comments

Weak Logos: Often lack evidence or clear reasoning.

Weak Ethos: No author credibility is usually established.

Weak Pathos: Emotional appeal may be shallow, cliché, or absent altogether.

Example: "Best day ever!!! 😍 🌀" — not built to convince, just to share.

4. Spam or Clickbait Writing

Weak Logos: Often uses illogical or misleading claims.

Weak Ethos: Comes from untrustworthy or unknown sources.

Weak Pathos: Manipulates with over-the-top language, not genuine emotion.

Example: "You won't believe what happened next!" — empty of real substance.

5. Basic Weather Reports or Traffic Updates

Weak Logos: Present facts but don't explain causes or implications.

Weak Ethos: Writer or announcer rarely emphasized as a credible authority.

Weak Pathos: Neutral tone, no emotional appeal.

Example: "Chance of rain: 60%. Drive time to downtown: 35 minutes."

30. Essential Argument Elements

Add a warrant. Possible responses are presented sentence-wise for clarity, and to illustrate to the writer the process of *construction* of an argument paragraph. It may be easier in the drafting stage to write sentences individually with this visual representation. This shows that argument paragraphs are constructed with specific elements, like bricks in a wall. It may be easier to create your warrant if you're looking at a list of sentences that you need to bring together conceptually rather than at a half-constructed paragraph you need to finish.

1. Claim: Reading fiction improves empathy.
   Evidence: A 2013 study in *Science* found that people who read literary fiction performed better on empathy tests.
   Warrant: Literary fiction often explores complex characters and emotions, requiring readers to imagine others' perspectives, which strengthens their ability to empathize in real life.
2. Claim: Handwriting notes aids memory better than typing.
   Evidence: Research from Princeton University shows that students who handwrite notes retain more information than those who type.
   Warrant: Handwriting forces students to process and rephrase information in their own words, deepening understanding and memory formation, unlike typing, which often encourages verbatim transcription.
3. Claim: Unexpected climates threaten global food supply.
   Evidence: Rising temperatures and extreme weather have already decreased crop yields in parts of Africa and South Asia.
   Warrant: Crops rely on stable temperatures and predictable weather patterns; when these shift, plants become less productive or fail entirely, reducing available food.
4. Claim: Social media can damage self-esteem.
   Evidence: Teens who spend more time on image-focused platforms like Instagram report lower self-confidence.
   Warrant: Constant exposure to curated, idealized images can cause users to compare themselves negatively to others, leading to diminished self-worth.
5. Claim: Music education supports academic success.
   Evidence: Students involved in music programs often score higher on standardized math and reading tests.

Warrant: Music training enhances cognitive skills such as memory, pattern recognition, and concentration, which directly support performance in academic subjects.

6. Claim: Learning a second language enhances brain function.
Evidence: Bilingual individuals show greater cognitive flexibility and problem-solving skills in multiple studies.
Warrant: Managing two languages strengthens the brain's ability to switch tasks, focus attention, and think critically, which boosts overall mental agility.

7. Claim: Sleep deprivation reduces productivity.
Evidence: A study by the CDC found that workers who sleep less than six hours per night are significantly less efficient on the job.
Warrant: Sleep is essential for attention, memory, and decision-making; without it, cognitive performance suffers and work efficiency drops.

8. Claim: Urban green spaces improve mental well-being.
Evidence: People who spend time in city parks report lower stress levels and improved mood.
Warrant: Nature exposure calms the nervous system, reduces cortisol (the stress hormone), and offers mental relief from overstimulating urban environments.

9. Claim: Meditation can lower stress levels.
Evidence: Hundreds of scientific studies have found that a 20-minute daily practice of mindfulness meditation results in noticeable improvement in stress and well-being in just two weeks.
Warrant: Mindfulness meditation trains the mind to rest and increases the mind-body connection, which reduces emotional reactivity and promotes a state of calm.

10. Claim: Conserving wildlife habitats preserves biodiversity and keeps the ecosystem well-calibrated.
Evidence: Protecting nature means species survival rates improve and ecosystems remain balanced.
Warrant: Each species plays a role in the ecological system; when their habitats are preserved, interdependent relationships continue functioning, preventing collapse or imbalance.

31. Additional Argument Elements

Add backing, rebuttal (both parts), and qualifier. End with a concluding sentence.

1. Reading fiction improves empathy (*claim*). A 2013 study in *Science* found that people who read literary fiction performed better on empathy tests (*evidence*). Literary fiction invites readers to step into others' emotional experiences, building understanding and compassion (*warrant*). Psychologists agree that mental simulation, imagining others' perspectives, is key to empathic development (*backing*). Some argue that watching films or documentaries also fosters empathy (*rebuttal*). While visual media may help, reading demands deeper cognitive engagement and reflection, which enhances emotional insight more effectively (*response*). Although not all fiction has this effect, literary fiction especially tends to challenge readers to understand nuanced characters (*qualifier*). For those looking to grow their empathy, reading fiction is a powerful and evidence-based tool.

2. Handwriting notes aids memory better than typing (*claim*). Research from Princeton University shows that students who handwrite notes retain more information than those who type (*evidence*). Handwriting forces students to process and rephrase information, which helps embed it in long-term memory (*warrant*). Cognitive scientists have shown that active engagement with material, rather than passive transcription, leads to stronger recall (*backing*). Some argue that typing is faster and allows for more complete notes (*rebuttal*). However, completeness doesn't guarantee comprehension; handwritten notes may capture less but deepen understanding (*response*). While typing may be suitable for recording facts quickly, handwriting offers superior learning for conceptual material (*qualifier*). When it comes to remembering what matters, a pen still beats a keyboard.

3. Unexpected climates threaten global food supply (*claim*). Rising temperatures and extreme weather have already decreased crop yields in parts of Africa and South Asia (*evidence*). Crops depend on stable growing conditions; unpredictable climates disrupt planting, growth, and harvest (*warrant*). Agricultural reports from the UN and FAO confirm that climate instability affects food security worldwide (*backing*). Critics claim that technology and genetically modified crops can offset these challenges (*rebuttal*). While innovation helps, it cannot fully protect vulnerable regions from severe climate shocks (*response*). Although wealthier countries may adapt more easily, many developing nations remain at risk (*qualifier*). As the climate grows more volatile, ensuring global food security will demand both prevention and adaptation.

4. Social media can damage self-esteem (*claim*). Teens who spend more time on image-focused platforms like Instagram report lower self-confidence (*evidence*). Constant exposure to idealized images causes negative social comparison, especially in adolescents (*warrant*). Psychologists note that appearance-based comparison is a known trigger for low self-worth and anxiety (*backing*). Some suggest that social media also connects people and builds communities (*rebuttal*). While connection is possible, the dominant visual culture on many platforms often leads to pressure and insecurity instead (*response*). Although not every user experiences harm, vulnerable teens are particularly affected (*qualifier*). Social media, when overused or poorly managed, can become a serious risk to adolescent self-esteem.

5. Music education supports academic success (*claim*). Students involved in music programs often score higher on standardized math and reading tests (*evidence*). Learning music strengthens concentration, memory, and pattern recognition—skills that support academic achievement (*warrant*). Neurological studies show that music training activates brain regions involved in learning and language (*backing*). Some argue that time spent on music could be used for core subjects instead (*rebuttal*). However, music enhances—not detracts from—academic ability by sharpening the very skills used across subjects (*response*). While results may vary by student and program, the overall academic benefits of music are well-documented (*qualifier*). Music education isn't just an enrichment—it's an advantage in the classroom.

6. Learning a second language enhances brain function (*claim*). Bilingual individuals show greater cognitive flexibility and problem-solving skills in multiple studies (*evidence*). Switching between languages strengthens mental control and improves multitasking (*warrant*). Neuroscience confirms that bilingual brains show denser gray matter in regions linked to memory and reasoning (*backing*). Some believe that learning a second language is too difficult or time-consuming for most adults (*rebuttal*). While challenging, even partial language learning shows cognitive benefits and increases mental agility (*response*). Though outcomes depend on effort and exposure, language learning benefits people of all ages (*qualifier*). A second language doesn't just open doors—it sharpens the mind behind them.

7. Sleep deprivation reduces productivity (*claim*). A CDC study found that workers who sleep less than six hours per night are significantly less efficient on the job

(*evidence*). Lack of sleep impairs attention, memory, and decision-making—key factors in workplace performance (*warrant*). Medical experts consistently link sleep quality with cognitive performance and reaction speed (*backing*). Some argue that successful people often thrive on minimal sleep (*rebuttal*). Though exceptions exist, most people function far better with consistent, sufficient rest (*response*). While sleep needs vary slightly, chronic deprivation consistently undermines productivity (*qualifier*). For sharper thinking and better results, sleep isn't optional—it's essential.

8. Urban green spaces improve mental well-being (*claim*). People who spend time in city parks report lower stress levels and improved mood (*evidence*). Nature exposure soothes the nervous system and offers relief from urban overstimulation (*warrant*). Environmental psychologists have shown that even short exposure to green environments lowers cortisol levels (*backing*). Some argue that city parks are too small or crowded to provide real peace (*rebuttal*). Even brief access to greenery—trees, grass, or water—can deliver mental health benefits (*response*). While not a substitute for wilderness, well-designed green spaces can meaningfully enhance urban life (*qualifier*). In the midst of concrete and traffic, green spaces offer a much-needed breath for the mind.

9. Meditation can lower stress levels (*claim*). Hundreds of studies show that 20 minutes of mindfulness meditation daily improves stress and well-being in just two weeks (*evidence*). Meditation trains attention and reduces emotional reactivity, allowing the mind to reset (*warrant*). Clinical research supports meditation as a non-pharmaceutical tool for stress reduction and mood improvement (*backing*). Critics say meditation is difficult or impractical for busy people (*rebuttal*). Apps and guided sessions now make it easier than ever to practice meditation in short, effective bursts (*response*). While not everyone sees the same results, most practitioners report noticeable benefits with consistency (*qualifier*). For managing stress in a demanding world, meditation offers a simple, evidence-based solution.

10. Conserving wildlife habitats preserves biodiversity and keeps the ecosystem well-calibrated (*claim*). Protecting nature means species survival rates improve and ecosystems remain balanced (*evidence*). Each species contributes to ecological health; the loss of one can disrupt the entire system (*warrant*). Ecologists warn that biodiversity loss weakens ecosystem resilience and increases vulnerability to collapse (*backing*). Some argue that human development should take priority over habitat

conservation (*rebuttal*). Yet healthy ecosystems provide services humans rely on—clean water, pollination, and climate regulation (*response*). While development is sometimes necessary, it must be balanced with protection of key ecosystems (*qualifier*). Conserving habitats isn't just about saving animals—it's about sustaining life for all.

32. Oral Presentation Structure

Good [morning/afternoon], everyone.

All over the world, from our gritty construction sites to those magnificent royal palaces in nearly every country, people enjoy a bottle of Coke (*hook*). What began at a soda fountain in the late 1800s has survived all of the tests of time, and today, more than 125 years later, human beings just absolutely love Coca-Cola. Its delicious recipe is certainly the biggest reason for its massive success. But Coca-Cola is more than just bubbly flavored water. Coca-Cola is an amazing company due to its global brand power, commitment to innovation and sustainability, and its strong social and economic impact (*speech claim*).

The first reason this company is so amazing is its unbelievable global brand power (*transition, restate speech claim, Point 1*). When we think of iconic brands, Coca-Cola almost always comes to mind. It's one of the most recognizable and trusted names in the world. That classic red-and-white logo, the distinctive contour bottle, and the familiar taste are known in over 200 countries. It's a brand that has become a symbol of refreshment and joy—from major global events to the smallest neighborhood store. Year after year, it ranks among the top global brands, and that kind of loyalty doesn't happen by accident. This brand has harnessed the world, making it a truly remarkable company in itself (*restate point 1 and speech claim*).

But Coca-Cola isn't just coasting on a strong brand to make it amazing (*transition/restate Point 1, restate speech claim*). It's constantly innovating and evolving. Today, the company offers hundreds of beverage options, including low-calorie, organic, and plant-based drinks that reflect changing consumer tastes. It's also making real investments in sustainability. With fully recyclable bottles, refillable systems, and its "World Without Waste" initiative, Coca-Cola is working to collect and recycle every bottle or can it sells by the year 2030. The innovativeness toward social responsibility this brand offers sets it apart from the competition and bolsters its global brand power (*restate Point 2, connect to speech claim, restate Point 1*).

A global superpower brand and deep sense of social responsibility are model business characteristics of this amazing company. Beyond business, Coca-Cola has a meaningful impact on communities and economies (*restate Points 1 & 2, restate speech claim, transition, Point 3*). Its global network of bottling partners provides jobs for hundreds of thousands of people, supporting families and small businesses around the world. And it gives back—through clean water programs, youth entrepreneurship, disaster relief, and education initiatives. These efforts show that Coca-Cola is more than a socially conscious global brand. It's an unlikely force for positive change (*restate Points 1 & 2, refer subtly to speech claim, restate Point 3*).

From its global brand presence and environmental leadership to its deep social engagement, Coca-Cola stands out as a company that combines business success with lasting positive impact (*restate Points 1, 2, & 3*). So next time you catch a glimpse of that well-known bottled beverage, feel free to help yourself, comfortable in your choice and confident that you're supporting one of the most amazing companies on earth (*restate speech claim, end with call to action to support the company*).

Thank you.

35. Relevant Visual on Each Slide

Concept to communicate	Sketch/Idea for visual
Coca-Cola is one of the most recognizable and trusted brands in the world. Its iconic red-and-white logo, classic contour bottle, and consistent flavor are known in over 200 countries.	Well-recognized Coca-Cola item, such as old Coke bottle, Coke in multiple languages, or other icon-type visual Message: Coke is in a class by itself, and all over the world
The brand's strong identity has made it a symbol of happiness and refreshment, visible in everything from international sporting events to local convenience stores.	People of all walks of life smiling. Maybe people at a sporting event or a royal family member with a Coke bottle. Opportunity to build ethos by who is included in the images
Its placement among the top global brands year after year reflects the deep connection people have with the product and its messaging.	People having fun, maybe around a campfire with a guitar, and Coke. Message: Coke is part of all of the best times in life

36. The 3-5 Rule

1.

Concept to communicate	Text
Coca-Cola is one of the most recognizable and trusted brands in the world. Its iconic red-and-white logo, classic contour bottle, and consistent flavor are known in over 200 countries. The brand's strong identity has made it a symbol of happiness and refreshment, visible in everything from international sporting events to local convenience stores. Its placement among the top global brands year after year	Brand Power - Recognizable, trusted - 200 countries - Symbolizes happiness & refreshment - Broad visibility - Prominence reflects deep human connection

reflects the deep connection people have with the product and its messaging.	

2.

Concept to communicate	Text
Coca-Cola continues to grow through innovation and environmental responsibility. The company offers a wide variety of beverages, including low-calorie, organic, and plant-based options, showing its awareness of changing consumer preferences. It has also made major investments in sustainable packaging, including fully recyclable bottles and refillable systems. One of its major environmental programs, "World Without Waste," aims to collect and recycle a bottle or can for every one sold by 2030, reflecting a broader commitment to sustainability.	Innovation & Environmental Responsibility - Broad variety - Sustainable packaging - "World Without Waste" program - 2030

3.

Concept to communicate	Text
Coca-Cola plays a major role in supporting communities and economies around the world. Through its vast network of bottling partners, it provides hundreds of thousands of jobs and helps power local economies. In addition to its business contributions, Coca-Cola supports a range of social initiatives, such as funding clean water access, youth entrepreneurship, disaster relief, and education. These efforts demonstrate the company's wide-reaching influence not only as a business leader, but also as a contributor to global well-being.	Social Support - Gives jobs, powers local economies - Social initiatives - Demonstrate they care

37.   Aristotle's Trilogy

Answers vary.

❧

The End

www.ingramcontent.com/pod-product-compliance
Lightning Source LLC
Chambersburg PA
CBHW081500070526
44586CB00019B/2440